Dedicated to my family:
Allen, Greg, Laurie, Doug, and Glenn, without whose cookie eating and appreciating abilities, these recipes would never have been devised.

*To Barbara
mon amie
Marilou
2000*

COOKIE ORIGINALE

Collected and created for you by Marilou Tombin

AN AUTHORS GUILD BACKINPRINT.COM EDITION

Cookie Originale

Collected and Created for you

All Rights Reserved © 1970, 2000 by Marilou Tomblin

No part of this book may be reproduced or transmitted in any form or by any means, graphic, electronic, or mechanical, including photocopying, recording, taping, or by any information storage or retrieval system, without the permission in writing from the publisher.

AN AUTHORS GUILD BACKINPRINT.COM EDITION

Published by iUniverse.com, Inc.

For information address:
iUniverse.com, Inc.
620 North 48th Street, Suite 201
Lincoln, NE 68504-3467

www.iuniverse.com

Originally published by Nitty Gritty Books

ISBN: 0-595-13186-7

Printed in the United States of America

Table of Contents

Cookies Are An Edible Art 1
Who Cooks Cookies? 2
How Does a Cookie Grow? 3
Pans and Other Indispensible Utensils 5
Basic Cookie Wisdom 6
How to Use Cookie Originale 7
Storing and Mailing Your Cookies 9
Drop Cookies 10
Molded Cookies 47
Bar Cookies 71
Rolled Cookies 109
Pressed Cookies 135
Refrigerator Cookies 147
Et Cetera Cookies 162
What Equals What 177
Gilding the Lily — Icings and Frostings 178
How to Vary Everything or Substitutes 179

Cookies Are An Edible Art

Cookie Originale is more than a collection of recipes. It is a philosophy of an art to be practiced. These recipes are meant to persuade, coax, encourage, and lovingly convince everyone of the true values and deep satisfaction derived from the making, giving, and eating of cookies. Particularly cookies that are your own creations.

Cookies are worth making if only to have the kitchen smell delightful. Cookies can be devoured almost as soon as they are put on the cooling racks, they can be stored to mellow, or when cool can be iced and decorated to make them pretty.

I have mixed, baked, and tasted all the cookies in this book. In some, the ingredients are standard but I urge you to make changes of your own or to use my suggested variations. Other recipes I have created or discovered for particular diets and situations. These depend on more unusual ingredients and preferences.

The more you use these recipes and enjoy the compliments of family and friends, the more you will want to be original yourself.

Who Cooks Cookies?

As long as the Human Race has had ovens (which goes back to prehistoric times in many Cultures) we have had cookies which are little bits of savory dough. Some think that cookies were first made attractive when they were used as religious offerings to the gods, particularly by the families who could not afford a sheep or a goat to bring to the altar. We know for certain that decorated cookies have figured in religious folk art for many thousands of years. Since cookies keep well they have been important to religious celebrations where labor is forbidden on feast days. Although certain traditions have lost their significance, cookies have not lost their popularity.

Not every country has a word equivalent for cookie. They are not labeled as easily as cakes and pies. Often a particular cookie has its own proper name such as *Madeleines,* French (a filled scallop shaped tea cake) or *Meringues* (egg white puffs) or *Springerli* (an imprinted white crusted German Christmas cookie). We of course have Brownies, Gingersnaps, and Fig Newtons which might all need footnotes of explanation in some ensuing century. What we Americans call "cookie" is called a "biscuit" in England and the Dominions.

The cookie's long and universal past encourages creativity. Just as a person plays or sings and interprets the music, so you can take a recipe and produce, improvise, and expand. The most important part of **Cookie Originale** is you. Every batch can be your original creation.

How Does A Cookie Grow?

All cookies are made with some kind of grain (even crushed graham crackers), something to bind them, and baked. Beyond this the variations are limitless. You will find cookies with ingredients from almonds to zwiebach and cookies for every occasion from children's lunches to gourmet feasts. Some are considered healthful with natural dried fruits, raw sugar, and whole wheat flour; while others include chocolate, Brandy, or confectioners' sugar. The choice is yours.

The sections of this book are organized into the six major methods of mixing and forming cookies. For substitutions refer to "How to Vary Everything" on page 179. Use your own tastes and preferences for such additions as raisins, nuts, dates, and spices as they do not alter the fundamental structure of the cookie. I sometimes specify vanilla sugar which is sugar in which a vanilla bean has been stored. If you like vanilla flavor you may wish to use it more often.

For those who live in high altitudes (over 4500 feet) you will need to increase oven temperature at least 25 degrees and often you will need to decrease baking powder from 3/4 to 1/2 teaspoon or in that ratio. You will also need to decrease baking soda in the same proportion.

Cookie watching is most important to cookie growing. Know your oven, your recipe, instructions, and don't worry about taking a peek. Cookies bake quickly so stay around and sniff and look. You may want your originales to be crispier than mine. It's your cookie.

Pans And Other Indispensible Utensils

Must Have:

2 Teflon cookie sheets	3 graduated mixing bowls
1 Teflon jelly roll sheet	4 graduated measuring spoons
3 wire racks for cooling	2 wooden spoons
1 9x9x2 inch Teflon pan	2 measuring cups (2 cup size)
1 8x10x2 inch rectangular pan	2 teaspoons

1 egg beater	wax paper
1 triple sifter	aluminum foil
1 wide spatula	plastic film wrap
1 rolling pin	plastic sandwich bags
cookie cutters	coffee cans

Nice to Have:

grater (orange rind)	double boiler (melting chocolate)
10x16 inch pan	more cookie cutters
electric mixer	kitchen scissors — cutting dried fruit
pastry brush	grinder — for fruit and nuts
	cookie jars

Basic Cookie Wisdom

If possible keep all cookie baking materials together. Put measuring spoons in the measuring cups, nested in bowls on top of the wire cooling racks placed on the cookie sheet (like a tray). All ingredients blend together better if they are at room temperature. Butter and margarine are easier to cream when left out of the refrigerator at least an hour. Butter and margarine are especially easy to measure if you think in terms of one cup equals two sticks or one-half pound. If you need to measure less than a cup of vegetable shortening (for example 3/4 cup) fill the measuring cup with 1/4 cup water and then spoon the shortening in until the water level reaches the 1 cup mark.

When measuring honey or molasses measure the shortening first and then the honey in the same cup. It won't stick as much. To make honey or molasses flow more easily warm them in the jar with the lid off in a pan of hot water. When melting chocolate squares or chocolate bits place the chocolate on a piece of aluminum foil in the top of a double boiler. Aluminum foil is also good to use on top of a cookie sheet since you can make up several batches while cookies are baking and clean-up is minimized. Wax paper is good to use on your counter and under your cooling racks to catch all crumbs. When greasing cookie sheets use vegetable shortening (it's unsalted) on a small piece of wax paper. Coat raisins or chopped dates with a little flour to help distribute them evenly in the dough.

When mixing drop cookies or bar cookies (the others you often refrigerate) preheat your oven while assembling and mixing. Anything that makes it easier makes it more fun to be creative.

**How To Use Cookie Originale -
There's A Cookie For Every Occasion**

This book is divided into six major sections according to preparation methods and a seventh section called *Et Cetera Cookies* is for cookie non-conformists.

An annotation written on each recipe tells you something special about the cookie. You will find that each recipe has temperature, baking time, and yield carefully recorded although these will vary with your own particular equipment and desires.

The quickest way to find a particular recipe will be to look in the Index. The right cookie will be the one that suits your fancy.

Storing And Mailing Your Cookies

Some cookies never see the light of another day, but some cookies improve if left to mellow. Cookie jars are gay and pretty, but a coffee can with a plastic lid or a glass jar can be used just as well. Keep crisp cookies in a tin with a loose lid and slip the cookies back into the oven if they gather too much moisture. Keep moist cakey cookies in a tin with a tight cover. Slices of apple changed from time to time will keep them delicious. Cookies made with honey, corn syrup, or molasses stay moist and keep longer than other kinds. Cookies with chopped fruit and spices should be made ahead of time to mellow. Bar cookies may be kept in the pan and thus transported to picnics or pot luck suppers. Paper plates covered with plastic wrap make an airtight disposable dish and plastic bags are ideal for the daily lunch box.

Baked cookies when cooled, may be stored in plastic freezer containers in your freezer compartment up to twelve months. It is best to thaw in the covered container to keep out moisture. Unbaked cookies and dough may be appropriately wrapped and kept up to six months in the freezer.

Bar cookies and molded cookies mail the best and especially ones with spices and fruits. Wrap in layers, use aluminum foil and plastic wrap to further seal off air. Pack the box tightly to keep cookies from moving around. Use sturdy boxes and write "Perishable-Food" on the package. For overseas mailing it is best to consult your Post Office for regulations.

Drop Cookies

Historically these were probably the first cookies — little bits of dough that could be baked and eaten quickly. They are still the most versatile, fastest, and sometimes the easiest.

Method: Mix all ingredients in one bowl. Cream shortening in a large bowl (until soft) using a wooden spoon. Gradually add sugar or sweetening and continue to cream. Add egg and flavoring if specified. Beat until smooth. Add sifted dry ingredients. Fold in the special additions last (nuts, fruit, etc.). Drop by rounded teaspoonsful and push with another teaspoon. Place dough about two inches apart on baking sheet (twelve to a sheet).

Hints: Chill dough to keep from overspreading. Peak up dough to keep shape. Remove from pan with wide spatula. Cool on wire racks. Most of these cookies can be dressed up by using one of the icings on page 178.

Carob Chip Cookie

Cream	½ cup butter or margarine
	¾ cup raw sugar
Beat in	1 egg
	1 tsp. vanilla
Sift & Add	1 cup pastry stone ground whole wheat flour
	½ tsp. baking soda
	½ tsp. salt
Mix well	
Stir in	1 cup carob chips*
	½ cup coarsely chopped nuts (your favorite)

Drop by well rounded half-teaspoonful on greased baking sheet. Bake at 375F for 10-12 minutes. * Buy at Health Food Stores.

Carob is also known as St. John's Bread. It has been a nutritious source of food grown in the Mediterranean area since Biblical times. The tree is widely grown in California where it can be recognized by the long brown pod hanging from the branches.
(4 dozen cookies)

This new recipe is sure to be a favorite with the teenagers in your home. The cookies taste like rich Dutch chocolate chip cookies, yet contain no cocoa or chocolate. Think how great it will be not to worry about your teenager's complexion.

Mandarin Chocolate Bits

Cream	1 cup butter or margarine
	½ cup granulated sugar
	½ cup orange honey
	1 3 oz. pkg. cream cheese (softened)
Add	2 slightly beaten eggs
	2 Tbsp. grated orange peel
	2 tsp. vanilla
Beat well	
Sift &	2 cups flour
Add	1 tsp. salt
Stir in	1 cup semi-sweet chocolate chips

Drop by spoonful on lightly greased sheet and bake at 350F for 10-12 minutes.
(4-5 dozen cookies)

These cakey cookies combine the tangy flavor of orange peel with the rich flavor of chocolate chips. The longer you keep them in the cookie tin, the more they mellow.

Sydney Biscuits

Cream	½ cup butter
	¾ cup granulated sugar
Add &	1 egg
Beat	1 tsp. vanilla
	1 cup coconut (fine and dry)
Sift &	1 cup flour
Add	1 tsp. baking powder
	1/8 tsp. salt

Spoon onto greased cookie sheet and flatten with bowl of spoon. Cook at 350F for 7 minutes. Leave on tray to cool a few minutes before removing.

(4 dozen cookies)

American Cookie - Australian Biscuit. Try this coconut biscuit which originated "Down Under".

Greg's Lemon Drops

Cream	1 cup butter or margarine
	1 cup confectioners' sugar
Add	1 egg
	1½ tsp. lemon juice
	1 tsp. lemon peel (grated)
Sift &	1¾ cup flour
Stir in	½ tsp. baking soda
	½ tsp. salt
	½ tsp. cream of tartar

Beat well. Drop onto greased cookie sheet. Sprinkle top with crushed lemon drops. Bake at 375F for 8-10 minutes. Watch carefully.
(3 dozen cookies)

If lemon is your family's favorite flavor as it is my son Greg's this rich, crisp double lemon cookie won't last long around your kitchen.

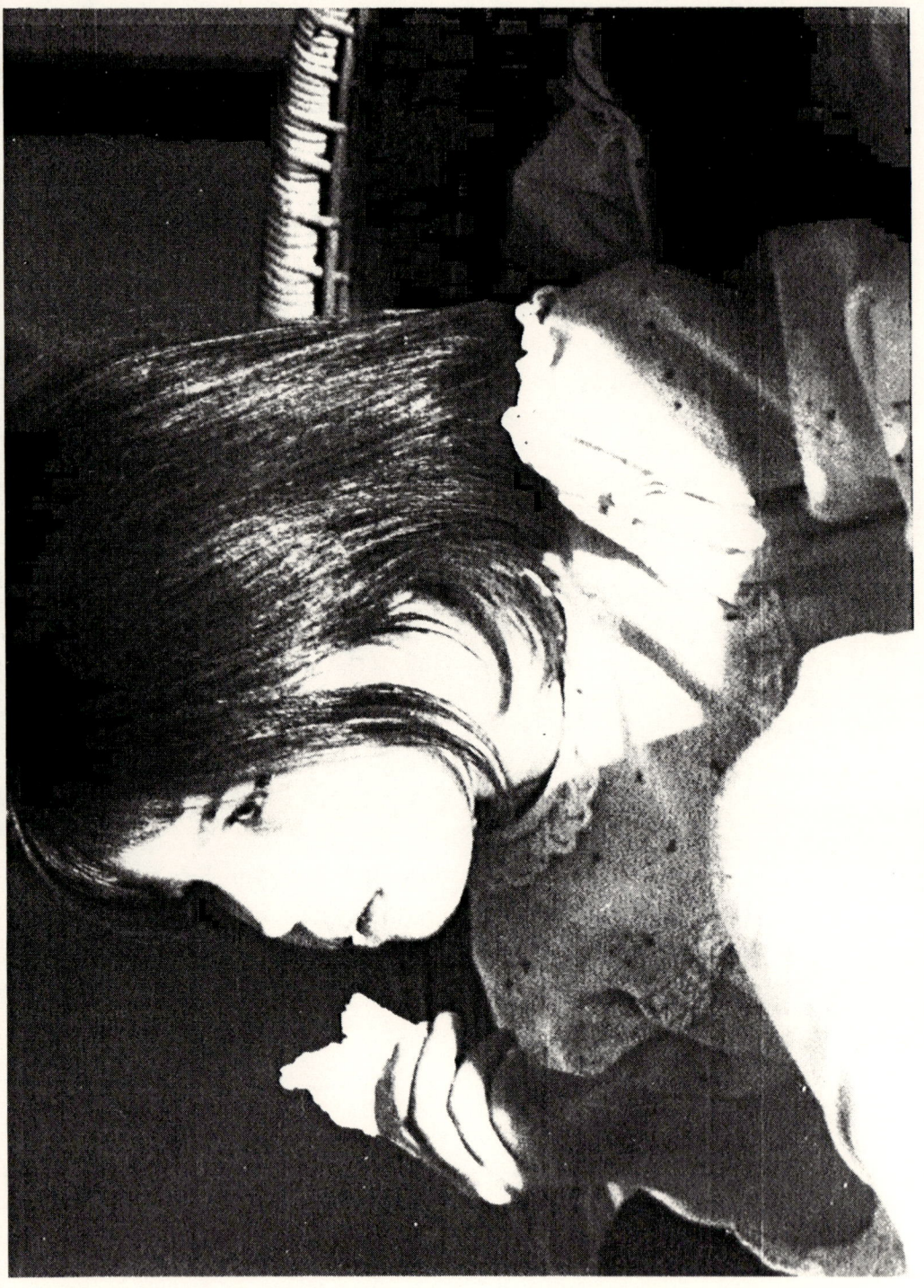

Birthday Party Cookies

Cream	¾ cup butter
	¾ cup confectioners' sugar
Add &	2 egg yolks
Beat	2 tsp. vanilla
Sift &	2 cups cake flour
Add	½ tsp. salt.
Add	drop of food coloring if you wish

Drop on ungreased cookie sheet. May be decorated with cherries, candies, whole nuts or your favorite tidbit before baking. May be iced after baking. Bake at 350F for 12-15 minutes.
(4 dozen cookies)

Purple - Green - Blue - Yellow
Pick your choice and catch a fellow.
Add the color to your taste,
See them disappear with haste.

Chocolate Fudgies

Cream	½ cup margarine
	1 cup brown sugar
Add	1 egg
Sift	1½ cups flour
	¼ tsp. baking soda
	¼ tsp. baking powder
	¼ tsp. salt

Add sifted ingredients alternately with

    ½ cup sour cream
    2 squares melted chocolate (cooled)
    1 cup coarsely chopped walnuts

Beat well and chill at least 1 hour. Drop by spoonsful on lightly greased sheet, making a small mound. Bake at 300F for 10-12 minutes. They should raise but not spread. Cool and ice with Glossy Icing which is made by creaming the following to spreading consistency: 1¾ cup sifted confectioners' sugar, 1 Tbsp. cream, 1 tsp. almond flavoring and 1 tsp. vanilla flavoring.
(4 dozen cookies)

Yummy good chocolate and rich sour cream combine to make these frosted favorites.

Carob Bean Islands

Cream	½ cup butter or margarine
	1 cup Kleen raw sugar
Add &	1 egg
Beat	1 tsp. vanilla
	½ cup milk
Sift &	1½ cups flour
Stir in	1 tsp. baking powder
	¼ tsp. salt
	½ cup carob powder*
Add	1 cup coconut (fine and dry)

Stir well. Raisins or finely chopped dates may be added.
Drop by spoonsful on greased baking sheet. Bake at 375F for 10-12 minutes. * Buy at Health Food Stores.
(4 dozen cookies)

Healthful for children because it tastes like chocolate but isn't. Let them help make these. There is no melting of chocolate.

Mother's Persimmon Cookies

Cream	½ cup shortening
	½ cup granulated sugar
	½ cup brown sugar
Blend in	1 cup ripe persimmon pulp
	(about 2 large persimmons)
	1 tsp. baking soda
Add	1 beaten egg
Sift & Stir in	2½ cups flour
	½ tsp. salt
	½ tsp. cinnamon
	½ tsp. nutmeg
	½ tsp. cloves
Add	1 cup raisins
	1 cup chopped walnuts

Drop on greased cookie sheet and bake at 375F for 15 minutes. Store in tightly covered tin, improving the flavor. Healthy Hint Substitute: Use 1 cup of raw sugar in place of other sugars. Use 1 cup of crushed graham crackers in place of 1 cup of flour.
(6 dozen cookies)

This is a family tradition at Thanksgiving time. You'll love them even if you don't like persimmons. We freeze persimmon pulp for later use. Excellent for mailing.

Pumpkin Eaters

Cream	½ cup butter or margarine
	1 cup brown sugar
Add	1 egg
Sift	1¾ cup flour
	½ tsp. salt
	1 tsp. cinnamon
	½ tsp. cloves
	½ tsp. nutmeg
Add alternately with	
	1 cup canned pumpkin
Stir in	1 cup all-bran
	½ cup chopped nuts
	½ cup seedless raisins

Drop by spoonful on greased cookie sheet. Bake at 375F for 12-15 minutes.
(4 dozen cookies)

Great for Halloween and for children who can't sit and wait for Thanksgiving dessert.

Honey Hermits

Cream	½ cup shortening
	1 cup honey
	½ cup brown sugar
Add	2 well beaten eggs
	3 Tbsp. milk
Sift &	2½ cups flour
Add	1 tsp. baking soda
	½ tsp. allspice
	½ tsp. cinnamon
Stir in	1 cup seedless raisins
	1 cup currants
	1 cup chopped dates
	1 cup chopped nuts

Drop onto greased cookie sheet. Bake at 400F for 10-12 minutes. (7 dozen cookies)

Bite size fruit cakes is what this recipe tastes like. For even more nutrition, subsitute whole wheat flour in place of white. This recipe keeps or mails well.

Banana-Honey Bumps

Cream	½ cup butter or margarine
	1 cup honey
Add	½ cup mashed banana (1 medium)
Sift	1½ cups flour
	½ tsp. baking powder
	1 tsp. baking soda
	½ tsp. salt
	½ tsp. cinnamon
	¼ tsp. nutmeg

Add alternately with
    ½ cup sour cream

Chill overnight or put in freezer one-half hour. Drop by teaspoon on lightly greased cookie sheet. Bake at 350F for 10-15 minutes. (4 dozen cookies)

The secret of the subtle flavor is chilling the dough. The banana and honey give the cookies a gorgeous golden glow.

Saucy Apple Cookies

Cream	1 cup butter or margarine
	2 cups brown sugar (raw sugar may be used)
Beat in	2 eggs
Stir in	2 cups moist applesauce (1 16-oz. can)
Sift &	3 cups flour
Stir in	1 tsp. baking soda
	1 tsp. salt
	1 tsp. nutmeg
	1 tsp. cloves
	1 tsp. cinnamon
Add	1 cup Grape Nuts
	1 cup raisins

Chill at least an hour or overnight. Drop on lightly greased cookie sheet. Bake at 375F for 5-8 minutes.
(6 dozen cookies)

Elementary school children can mix these up and then pack them to school for a treat in their lunches.

Homespun Oatmeal Cookies

Cream	½ cup margarine
	1¼ cup Kleen raw sugar
Add	2 eggs
	6 Tbsp. molasses
Sift &	1¾ cups whole wheat flour
Stir	1 tsp. baking soda
	1 tsp. baking powder
	1 tsp. cinnamon
Stir	2 cups rolled oats (not instant)
in	1 cup raisins

Drop on greased cookie sheet. Bake at 325F for 10-12 minutes. (5 dozen cookies)

Dunked in milk, these make a wonderful bedtime snack.

Honey Hugs

Cream	½ cup shortening
	1 cup honey
Stir in	1½ cups flour (whole wheat preferred)
	½ tsp. soda
	½ tsp. salt
	½ tsp. cinnamon
Add alternately with	
	2 cups Granola*
	4 Tbsp. sour milk
Stir in	½ cup chopped filberts
	(may use more if desired)

Drop on greased baking sheet and bake at 350F for 15 minutes.
* Health food store mixture of oatmeal, grains, and a little coconut etc. If you can't find Granola use Swiss Muesli.
(3 dozen cookies)

Everyone loves a Hug. They are so healthful for you.

Energy Cookies

Cream	½ cup shortening
	1 cup brown sugar (raw sugar if possible)
Add	1 unbeaten egg
	½ tsp. vanilla
Sift &	½ cup wheat flour
Mix in	½ tsp. soda
	2 tsp. baking powder
	¼ tsp. salt
Add	½ cup coconut
	½ cup oatmeal
	1 cup wheat germ
	1 cup corn flakes

Add a little water if needed to make dough hold together. Bake at 350F on greased cookie sheet for 10 minutes. Let set before removing.
(5 dozen cookies)

Your family will enjoy the nutritious flavor and varied texture of this cookie. Serve them with fruit for dessert, or send them packing in lunches.

Sutter's Gold Nuggets

Cream   1 cup butter
               1½ cups brown sugar
Add   3 eggs (slightly beaten)
Beat above mixture well
Add   1 tsp. baking soda dissolved in 1 Tbsp. water
               1 cup chopped raisins
               1 cup chopped walnuts
Add   2 cups sifted flour
Mix well
Drop onto greased baking sheet and bake at 400F for 8-10 minutes.
(6 dozen cookies)

This is truly "Grandma's Recipe". The golden nuggets mail exceptionally well.

Lacy Doilies

Stir Together	2½ cups rolled oats
	2½ cups brown sugar
	3 Tbsp. flour
	1 tsp. salt
Melt & Stir in	½ pound shortening
Add & Stir in	1 egg slightly beaten
	1 tsp. vanilla

Let coagulate about 5 minutes. Bake on ungreased cookie sheet at least 2 inches apart (they spread) for 5 minutes at 375F. Let cookies cool on the sheet for at least 2 minutes. Remove carefully with wide spatula and cool on rack. (They fall apart if moved too soon.) They should look translucent and truly lacy and brittle. I like to bake them in small batches just before needed and I keep a bowl of the dough in the refrigerator for instant treats.
(5 dozen cookies)

The delicate lacy texture of this cookie demands immediate consumption. Be sure to follow directions carefully, technique is important.

Elegante Macaroons

Work ½ pound of almond paste* in hands until soft.
Gradually add 1 cup granulated sugar
        3 egg whites
Knead above until paste has been absorbed.
Add until absorbed
        2 Tbsp. sifted cake flour
Add   ½ cup finely chopped glaced pineapple
        ½ cup chopped blanched almonds

Drop small teaspoonsful on ungreased wrapping paper or aluminum foil. Pat tops lightly with fingers dipped in cold water. Bake at 300F for 24-30 minutes. Will not stick if you use aluminum foil. If paper is used steam off by wet towel method. Store in covered jar with a piece of fresh bread. * Buy from bakery or make with 2 cups finely ground almonds (not toasted), 1½ cups confectioners' sugar, ¼ cup egg whites (unbeaten), and 2 tsp. almond extract. Mold into ball and age tightly covered in refrigerator.

(3-4 dozen cookies)

Almond paste is the base to these tricky but heavenly macaroons. Follow directions carefully.

Hollywood Meringues

Beat until	2 egg whites
Soft peaks	½ tsp. vanilla
Form	¼ tsp. salt
Gradually	1 cup confectioners' sugar
Add	(Beating until stiff)
Fold in	2 cups crushed corn flakes
	½ cup chopped nuts (fine)
	1 cup shredded coconut

Drop by heaping teaspoonsful on well greased cookie sheet. Top each with candied cherry or filbert. Bake at 300F for 20 minutes or until lightly toasted. Cool slightly before removing to keep shape.
(2 dozen cookies)

Glamorous cookies that are almost candy. Try using left-over yolks in Wilshire Tea Cookies. They're good too.

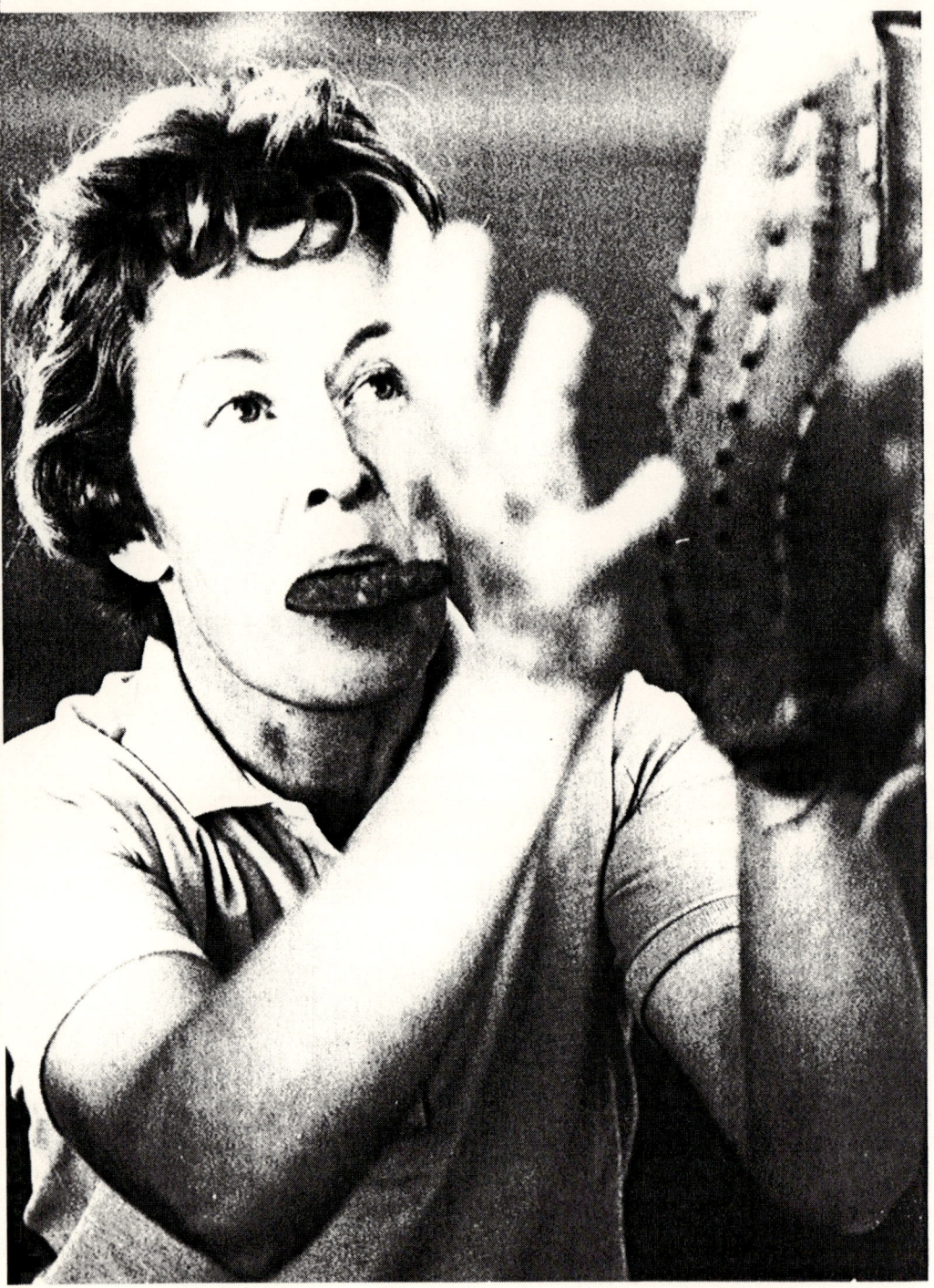

Classic Sugar Cookies

Cream	½ cup butter or margarine
	½ cup granulated sugar
Add	1 egg
	1 tsp. vanilla
Sift &	1 1/8 cup flour
Stir in	¼ tsp. baking soda
	½ tsp. salt

After mixing well drop by spoonful on lightly greased cookie sheet. Bake at **350F** for 8-10 minutes. Cool slightly before removing to wire racks.

Variations on the Classic Theme:

1. Sprinkle with cinnamon sugar before baking (1 tsp. cinnamon and 2 Tbsp. sugar). 2. Sprinkle with coarse colored sugar before baking or stud with little candies. 3. Stir ½ cup of your favorite chopped nuts into dough. 4. After baking and while hot cover with an orange glaze (4 Tbsp. sugar and 2 Tbsp. orange rind). 5. After baking, cool and spread with frosting. See Gilding the Lily. 6. Press cinnamon red-hots into dough before baking. 7. Sprinkle tops with crushed corn flakes. Top with cherry and bake.

(3 dozen cookies)

Need a variety of cookies? Double or triple the recipe and then divide into smaller portions and try any or all of the variations suggested. You will be delighted.

The Bride's Kisses

Beat until soft and moist
    ½ cup egg whites (about 5)
Stir in and beat in gradually
    1½ cups granulated sugar
    ½ tsp. salt
    1 tsp. Grand Marnier (or orange liquor)
Fold in   2½ cups moist coconut

Drop by rounded teaspoonsful 2 inches apart on ungreased brown wrapping paper cut to fit the baking sheet (grocery bags are fine). Cookies may be decorated with half an orange fruit jelly (gum drop) or small dainty candies. Bake at 325F for 10-15 minutes. Should be delicately crusty. When baked take brown paper with cookies and lay on a wet towel for 2-3 minutes. Carefully slip off cookies with a wide spatula (pancake turner type) and cool on wire racks.

(3 dozen cookies)

Planning a bridal shower? These delicate, light and airy cookies are excellent with champagne - just a hint of orange.

Peanut Palominos

Cream	1 cup brown sugar
	½ cup margarine
Add	1 lightly beaten egg
	½ tsp. vanilla
Mix thoroughly	
Stir in	½ cup thick sour cream
	alternately with sifted dry ingredients
Sift &	1½ cups flour (substitute whole wheat if desired)
Add	¼ tsp. salt
	¼ tsp. baking powder
	½ tsp. baking soda
Add	¾ cup chopped Spanish peanuts

Chill dough one hour. Drop from teaspoon on lightly greased sheet. These cookies look better if they don't spread out but stand up like little cakes. Bake at 375F for 10 minutes. When cool frost with Palomino Icing and decorate with a peanut. Palomino Icing: Mix ¼ cup soft peanut butter, 1 Tbsp. soft margarine with 1 cup sifted confectioners' sugar, a little at a time. Stir in 1 tsp. vanilla. Stir in 1-2 Tbsp. of hot water a little at a time until mixture is of spreading consistency.
(5 dozen cookies)

Children will like this fancy snack before bedtime with milk.

Carob Puffs

Beat   2 egg whites
              ¼ tsp. salt
              ½ tsp. vanilla
Until peaks form
Gradually add - beating until peaks are stiff
              1 cup confectioners' sugar
              3 Tbsp. carob powder
Fold in   1 cup finely chopped filberts

Drop by heaping teaspoon on well greased cookie sheet. Bake at 300F for 20 minutes (peek at 15 minutes). Cool slightly before removing from pan.
(2 dozen cookies)

These dainty and light cookies are great for those who like but can't eat chocolate. The recipe is easily doubled for a party.

Now Cookies

Cream	½ cup butter or margarine
	8 oz. grated cheddar cheese (nippy or sharp)
Work in well	
Blend in	½ cup sifted flour
	¼ tsp. garlic salt
	¼ tsp. celery salt
	¼ tsp. onion salt
Add	3 cups Kelloggs All Bran, shredded type

Drop by teaspoonsful on ungreased baking sheet. Bake at 325F for 15-20 minutes. Serve hot and enjoy now, but tasty anytime. (4 dozen cookies)

Great with cocktails, soups, and salads. Mix up, bake, and serve immediately. Change the herbs and salts to your taste.

Breakfast Cookies

Cream	½ cup margarine
	1 cup Kleen raw sugar
Add	1 tsp. vanilla
	1 beaten egg
	½ cup raisins
	½ cup drained crushed pineapple
Add	2 cups Instant Roman Meal Cereal
	½ tsp. salt
	1 tsp. baking soda

Mix well. Drop from teaspoon onto greased cookie sheet 2 inches apart. Bake at 375F for 10-12 minutes.
(4 dozen cookies)

When you can't stop for breakfast, take these along. They have everything to take you through the morning.

Coffee Toffees

Cream	½ cup margarine or butter
	2/3 cup brown sugar
Add	2 Tbsp. instant coffee
Add	1 egg, slightly beaten
Add	¾ cup stone ground whole wheat flour
	¼ tsp. salt
	½ tsp. vanilla

Mix well. Drop by spoonsful onto very lightly greased cookie sheet. Put pecan half on top and bake at 350F for 10-12 minutes. Remove to cooling racks immediately.
(3 dozen cookies)

These quick and easy, crisp and buttery cookies are very tasty, especially when served with ice cream or fruit. The recipe is very easy to double for your child's birthday party.

Cashew Treats

Cream   ½ cup shortening
              ¾ cup Cashew butter (make your own in a blender or buy from health food store)
              ½ cup Kleen raw sugar
Add   ½ cup honey
Beat well
Beat &   2 eggs
Add   1 tsp. vanilla
Add   1 cup chopped dates
Sift and add alternately with ¼ cup milk
              2 cups stone ground flour
              2½ tsp. baking powder
              ½ tsp. salt
Blend well
Drop by spoonsful on greased baking sheet. Decorate with half cashew nut. Bake at 350F for 15 minutes.
(4 dozen cookies)

These soft and cakey treats mail or keep well in your cookie tin and they are so good for you.

Molded Cookies

These cookies are very much like drop cookies but they are stiffer and you mix by hand.

Method: Cream shortening and sugar and add other ingredients all in the same bowl. Use your hands to shape into balls or into other forms as the recipe indicates. These cookies are great favorites with children and young people who like to mold them like clay. When the cookies are baked they are sometimes rolled in powdered sugar and here again the assistance of the family makes it fun for all.

Doug's Karma Cookies

Cream	¾ cup safflower or soy oil
	1 cup Kleen Raw sugar*
Add	1 cup date sugar
Add	½ cup honey
	1 tsp. vanilla
Add	1 cup lightly toasted sesame seeds (untreated)
	½ cup coconut (shredded and unsweetened)

Slowly add in 4 parts

    2 cups stone ground whole wheat flour
    1-2 Tbsp. warm water

Form into balls. Flatten with a knife. Place on lightly greased cookie sheet. Bake at **350F** for 8-10 minutes. Let sit a minute before removing. * If you do not wish any sugar omit this ingredient and increase honey to 1 cup.
(4 dozen cookies)

How about trying a health food cookie? No eggs or leavening. Just nature's best go into these cookies created originally for my son.

Laurie's Loves - Butter Nut Crescents

Cream	1¾ stick (7/8 cup butter)
	4 Tbsp. confectioners' sugar
	1 tsp. vanilla
Add	1 tsp. water
Mix	1 cup flour (sifted)
	1 cup chopped walnuts
Add	1 more cup of sifted flour and mix until stiff

Shape in approximately 1-inch cocoons and bake in slow oven, 300F about 10-12 minutes. Roll in powdered sugar while warm. They should be well coated.
(80 cookies)

No eggs are required for these Prep School favorites. We suggest you make them a little larger if they are to travel via mail.

Navidados

Cream	1 cup butter
	(can be half butter, half margarine)
	¾ cup sifted confectioners' sugar
Add	1 tsp. vanilla
Sift & add	2 cups flour
Add	1 cup finely chopped filberts

Divide dough in half. Add 3 teaspoons powdered espresso coffee to half the dough. Roll each half into balls. Flatten with a glass dipped in confectioners' sugar. Bake on an ungreased cookie sheet at 300F for 30-35 minutes. Put ½ cup confectioners' sugar in a shallow soup dish and coat cookies with sugar while still hot.
(4 dozen cookies)

Created on a Christmas Eve afternoon. They are good immediately, or will keep well.

California Raisin Balls

Cream	1 cup margarine
	1½ cups granulated sugar
Mix in	2 tsp. grated lemon rind
	2 Tbsp. lemon juice
	1 egg
Sift & Stir	2½ cups flour
	½ tsp. salt
	½ tsp. baking powder
Add	2 cups raisins

Chill dough at least an hour. Roll dough into balls, then roll in granulated sugar. Bake at 375F for 8-10 minutes on ungreased sheet.
(6 dozen cookies)

No fancy ingredients, but oh so good and so easy too.

Christmas Treats

Cream	1 cup shortening
	½ cup granulated sugar
Add	2 egg yolks (beaten)
	2 tsp. finely chopped candied orange peel
	2 tsp. finely chopped citron
	2 tsp. lemon juice

Mix thoroughly

Sift &	2 cups cake flour
Stir in	1 tsp. salt

Chill until firm. Form into small balls. Dip in egg whites, then roll in finely chopped nuts. Place a candied cherry on top of each. Bake on greased cookie sheet at 325F for 15-20 minutes.
(3 dozen cookies)

Eliminate the last minute Christmas baking problem. Make these well in advance, pack in a tight tin box, and allow them to mellow .

Coconut Shaggies

Cream	1 cup butter or margarine
	¼ cup sifted confectioners' sugar
	2 tsp. vanilla
Stir in	1 Tbsp. water
Sift &	2 cups flour
Add	1 cup chopped pecans

Roll into 1-inch balls. Bake on ungreased sheet at 300F for 20 minutes. Your cookies should be delicately brown. Cool thoroughly before removing from pan. Dip in confectioners' frosting (Gilding the Lily page 178) and roll in white coconut or tinted coconut colors. To tint coconut add a few drops of food coloring to coconut in a covered jar. Shake until desired shade has been achieved.
(4 dozen cookies)

This recipe makes the perfect hostess gift when packed in an apothecary jar. Try coloring the coconut green at Christmas, or pastel tints at Easter. You will be pleasantly surprised with your talents.

Chocolate Munchies

Melt	½ cup margarine
	2 squares unsweetened chocolate
Cool slightly	
Blend in	2 cups granulated sugar
	2 eggs (beat well after each addition)
Add	½ cup chopped pecans
Sift &	2 cups cake flour
Add	2 tsp. baking powder
	½ tsp. salt

Chill at least 15 minutes. Form into balls and roll in granulated sugar. Place on greased cookie sheet two to three inches apart. Bake at 350F for 15 minutes. Remove from cookie sheet immediately.

Variations:

  Mocha Munchies - Add 2 Tbsp. instant coffee with butter and sugar in the initial blending. Roll in powdered sugar before baking.

  Coco-choc Munchies - Fold in ½ cup coconut and use walnuts instead of pecans.

(4 dozen cookies)

Like a crinkly cookie? Try these in contrast to butter cookies. The variations are temptingly good.

Jamey Pies - Almost Little Tarts

Cream	½ cup shortening
	½ cup brown sugar
	1 egg yolk
	½ tsp. vanilla
Sift &	1 cup flour
Stir in	¼ tsp. salt

Form into balls the size of a walnut. Dip into slightly beaten egg white and roll in 1 cup chopped walnuts. Place 1-inch apart on lightly greased cookie sheet. Bake at 375F for 5 minutes. Remove from oven and make indentations with teaspoon. Place dab of favorite jam in the little dents. Return to oven and bake 6-8 minutes longer. Remove from cookie sheet at once.
(2 dozen cookies)

For variety, use different types of jams or marmalade. This recipe is a favorite among the younger male set.

Shortbread - American Style

Cream	½ cup peanut butter crunchy style (soft)
	½ cup butter or margarine
	½ cup brown sugar
	½ cup granulated sugar
Add	1 egg
Sift &	1¼ cup flour
Stir in	½ tsp. baking powder
	½ tsp. salt

Stir mixture and form into balls the size of a walnut. Place on greased cookie sheet about 2 inches apart. Press ball down with knife and put a spanish peanut on top. Bake at **350F** for 12-15 minutes or until delicately brown.

(4 dozen cookies)

For the next Cub Pack meeting, the companion to this cookie is cider.

Butterscotch Flings

Cream	½ cup margarine
	1 cup brown sugar
Add	1 egg
	1 tsp. vanilla

Beat until light and fluffy.

Sift &	1 cup flour
Stir in	½ tsp. baking soda
	½ tsp. salt
Fold in	1 cup oatmeal
	½ cup pecans chopped
	1 cup coconut

Roll into 1-inch balls. Drop on greased cookie sheet. Flatten each cookie with glass dipped in flour. Bake at 325F for 10-12 minutes. Remove from pan immediately.
(4 dozen cookies)

Still another oatmeal cookie full of goodies that mails well.

Desert Date Rocks

Cream	1½ cups brown sugar
	1 cup vegetable shortening
Add	3 Tbsp. hot water
Beat well	
Add	1 cup sifted white flour
	1 cup whole wheat flour
	1 cup finely ground walnuts
	1 tsp. salt
	1 tsp. cloves
	1 tsp. cinnamon
Add	1½ cup chopped dates (coated with a little flour)

Mix well. Dough will be stiff. Mix with finger and hands and roll into 1-inch balls. If dough won't stick together add hot water sparingly. (Too much water makes cookies spread out and they loose their hard crunchy texture.) Place on greased cookie sheet. Bake at 350F for 15 minutes.
(5 dozen cookies)

Cookies should be hard and crunchy. Keeps well. Mails well. Keeps indefinitely if well hidden.

Brunch Cookies

Cream	2/3 cup margarine
	1 cup orange honey
Beat in	2 eggs
	4 tsp. grated orange rind
Beat in	2 cups whole wheat flour
	2 tsp. baking powder
	1 tsp. salt
Fold in	3 cups bran flakes
	1 cup raisins

Roll in 1-inch balls and place on lightly greased baking sheets. Flatten with glass dipped in sugar. Bake at 350F for 8-10 minutes. (4 dozen cookies)

A crisp, healthful treat full of raisins, bran, and honey. A light meal with a glass of milk for after school or bedtime snack.

Coconut Nutties

Brown slightly ½ cup butter or margarine in the top of a double boiler. Remove from heat and place ice water in bottom pan.
Add   ¾ cup brown sugar slowly and beat until fluffy
Add   1 tsp. vanilla
             1 cup sifted flour
             ½ tsp. baking soda
Mix well and roll into 1-inch balls. Sprinkle ½ cup coconut in a shallow dish and press balls into coconut. Place a macadamia nut or almond firmly into cookie on top of coconut. Place on lightly greased sheet. Bake at 250-275F for 30 minutes. This recipe can easily be doubled.
(2½ dozen cookies)

Goes nicely with tropical fruit. Hard and crunchy. Eggless.

The Other Almond Macaroons

Blend   ½ cup powdered sugar (sifted)
           2 Tbsp. flour (sifted)
           1 large egg white (unbeaten)
           ¼ tsp. almond flavoring
           ¼ tsp. baking powder
Add   4 ounces of finely ground almonds

Mix together until well blended. Wet hands and roll mixture into 1-inch balls. Place 2 inches apart on greased cookie sheet. Brush surface with cold water and press down with top of wet spoon. Bake at 300F for 20 minutes or until delicately brown but not hard.
(2 dozen cookies)

You don't need almond paste for this one. Great with ice cream and puddings. And so easy. Decorate to please your family.

Rice Almond Cakes

Sift   1 cup rice flour
               ½ cup granulated sugar
               ¼ tsp. salt
Mix in   2 cups ground blanched almonds
Work in 1/3 cup butter, no substitutes (softened)
Mix until smooth. Add a few drops of water if needed to hold together. Shape into 1-inch balls. Place on greased cookie sheet about 2 inches apart. Brush with egg yolk beaten with 1 Tbsp. water and put a small almond on top of each cookie. Bake at 350F about 15 minutes or until golden.
(2-3 dozen cookies)

The authentic Chinese ingredients make these not-too-sweet cakes a delight.

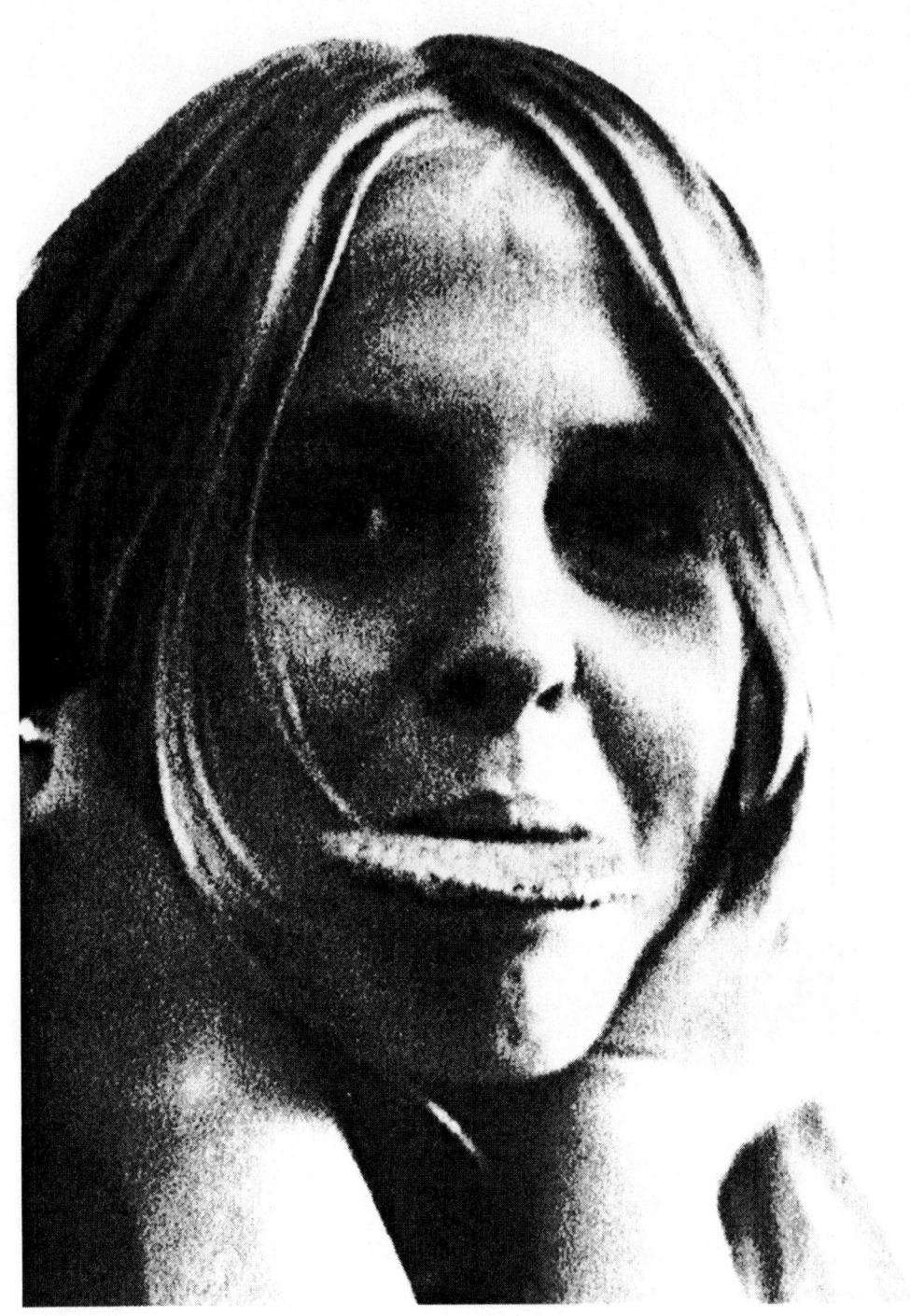

Piñonitas (Pine Nut Balls)

Cream   1 cup butter
             ½ cup confectioners' sugar
Add   1 tsp. vanilla
Mix until fluffy
Sift &   2 cups whole wheat pastry flour
Add   ½ cup chopped pine nuts

Roll into balls the size of walnuts. Place on ungreased cookie sheet. Bake at 300F for 30 minutes. Roll in ½ cup confectioners' sugar while still warm.
(4 dozen cookies)

This recipe of early California includes the deliciously different flavor of pine nuts.

Almond Butter Balls

Cream	½ cup almond butter*
	½ cup margarine
Cream in	1 cup Kleen raw sugar
Add	1 egg beaten
Add	1 cup stone ground whole wheat flour
	1 cup wheat germ
	½ tsp. baking powder
	½ tsp. salt

*Buy at health food store or make in blender or juicer. You may substitute ½ cup finely ground almonds and increase margarine to ¾ cup if you can't buy almond butter. Mix well and form into balls. Top with half a filbert. Place on ungreased cookie sheet. Bake 350F for 10 minutes. These are soft when you take them out but they harden.
(4 dozen cookies)

These will bring the compliments and they are good for you. Great for lunch boxes.

Bar Cookies

Bar cookies can be the easiest of all. Often they take no creaming, they are baked all at once, and need only to be cut into bars. They can be cut into small bars and iced for teas and special occasions or when divided into larger portions they can be served as a dessert topped with whipped cream or ice cream. Since they are rich with added fruits and nuts they are often made to be stored and served later.

Some bar cookies are made like drop cookies i.e. creaming, beating in eggs, adding sifted dry ingredients, and stirring in fruit or nuts. However, there are many variations of methods. They often have layers which give them even greater variety. Bar cookies are baked in a shallow pan, square or rectangle, usually one and a half to two inches deep. These cookies keep and travel well through the mail, in aluminum foil, or in a pan to picnic or pot luck. Grease and flour the pan and line with wax paper or foil for added ease in removing.

Kindness Cookies

Beat 3 eggs
Add 1 cup honey
Continue beating
Add 1 cup whole wheat stone ground flour
½ cup wheat germ
½ cup Roman Meal cereal
¼ tsp. salt
Mix well
Add ½ cup black mission figs (chopped)
½ cup raisins
½ cup chopped hazelnuts or filberts

Bake in two 9 x 9 well greased pans at 350F for 15-20 minutes. Cut, and after slightly cooled, roll in powdered sugar if desired. (6 dozen cookies)

On a diet? No sugar or shortening in these. Just natural foods so good for you. Great for the nibbler.

Family Brownies - A Traditional Cookie

Cream   ½ cup margarine
           1 cup granulated sugar
           3 Tbsp. carob powder

Sift & add in three parts
           2/3 cups flour
           1 tsp. baking powder
           ¼ tsp. salt

Add in two parts after first dry mixture
           2 eggs beaten
           ¼ cup milk
           1 tsp. vanilla

Beat well until fluffy

Fold in   1 cup coarsely chopped nuts
           1 cup of raisins for moistness if desired

Bake at 300F in greased 9x9 pan for 30 minutes. Cut while hot. Sprinkle with powdered sugar. If you want to frost, make carob powder icing as follows: 1 cup confectioners' sugar, 1 Tbsp. carob powder, 2 Tbsp. margarine, 1 Tbsp. cream; mix until smooth. (2-3 dozen cookies)

Little girls can make this one because you don't melt chocolate on the stove. Better for you than chocolate. Soft and caky too.

Status Brownies

Melt over	2 squares of unsweetened chocolate
Hot water	½ cup margarine
Beat in	1 cup sugar
	4 egg yolks
Sift &	¾ cup flour
Stir in	½ tsp. salt
	½ tsp. baking powder
Fold in	1 cup finely chopped almonds

Spread in well greased 9x9 pan. Bake for 30 minutes at 350F. Cut immediately into squares or diamonds.
(3 dozen brownies)

A good way to use up egg yolks. Substitute finely chopped filberts or walnuts for almonds if you prefer.

Charlie's Brownies

Beat	2 eggs until light and lemon colored
Add	½ cup granulated sugar
Sift &	¾ cup flour
Add	½ tsp. baking powder
	¼ tsp. salt
Melt	1 6 oz. pkg. of semisweet chocolate bits
	1/3 cup butter or margarine

Cool and add to the first mixture. Stir and mix well.

Add	1 tsp. vanilla
	1 cup chopped nuts

Put in greased 9x9 pan. Bake at 350F for 25 minutes. Cut while warm. Frost with peppermint icing, chocolate, or plain butter icing.
(3 dozen brownies)

Frost these teenage favorites with peppermint and see how fast they disappear.

Milk Chocolate Almond Bars

Cream   ½ cup soft shortening
              ½ cup firmly packed brown sugar
Sift &   1 cup flour
Mix in   ¼ tsp. salt

Press into well greased 9x9 pan. Bake at 350F for 20 minutes. Take out of oven. Sprinkle one package of milk chocolate bits immediately on hot bars. Spread evenly with spatula and add ½ cup slivered almonds. Place in warm but turned off oven for 5 more minutes. Cool. Cut into squares.

(3 dozen bars)

Need something quick and easy? This candy-like recipe will fill the requirements.

Panocha Cookies

Melt	¼ cup margarine
Add &	1 cup brown sugar
Beat	1 egg
	½ tsp. vanilla
Sift &	1 cup flour
Stir in	1 tsp. baking powder
	¼ tsp. salt
Add	1 pkg. (6 oz.) butterscotch bits
	½ cup chopped walnuts

Put in well greased 9x9 pan. Bake at 350F for 25 minutes. Be careful not to overbake. Cookies should be chewey.
(3 dozen cookies)

If you like a rich cookie and don't want chocolate, try these. Mails well also.

Luau Cookies

Mix Together	½ cup butter or margarine
	½ cup brown sugar
	1 cup sifted flour

Press and flatten in 9x12 pan. Bake 10 minutes in a 350F oven. Allow to cool slightly.

Beat & Spread with	2 beaten eggs
	3/4 cup honey
	1 tsp. vanilla
Add	1 cup moist coconut
	1 cup chopped macadamia nuts

Return to oven and bake 25-30 minutes until top layer is golden. Cool slightly and cut into squares.
(3-4 dozen cookies)

Macadamia nuts and coconut make these perfect for a Hawaiian feast.

Glenn's Grooveys

Cream	½ cup margarine
	½ cup brown sugar
	1 tsp. vanilla
Stir in	1 cup sifted flour
	½ cup Grape Nuts

When well mixed press evenly into bottom of greased 9x9 pan. Bake at 375F for 15 minutes or until golden. It is important to cool slightly. Melt 1 6-ounce pkg. milk chocolate pieces. Spread evenly over baked crust and sprinkle with additional ½ cup of Grape Nuts. Press down Grape Nuts a little so they don't loosen. Put back in oven for 5 minutes. Cut bars while still warm then cool completely before removing from pan. Take them to a picnic in the pan, they are great.

(3 dozen bars)

The Grape Nuts give this recipe a rich nutty flavor. Leave them in the baking pan for picnics or pot lucks.

Hop Scotch Squares

Cream	1 cup butter or margarine
	2 tsp. vanilla
	1½ cups brown sugar
Sift	1½ cups flour
	2 tsp. baking powder
	½ tsp. salt

Add above mixture alternately with ½ cup hot water.
Stir in 3 cups rolled oats.
Divide in half. Add 1 cup semi-sweet chocolate chips to one half. Spread this half in greased 9x9 pan. Add 1 cup butterscotch chips to other half and put this in another greased 9x9 pan. Bake at 375F for 30 minutes. Cut into squares and alternate on a dish or platter when serving.
(6 dozens squares)

This one is sure to please whether you mail it or take it with you on a picnic.

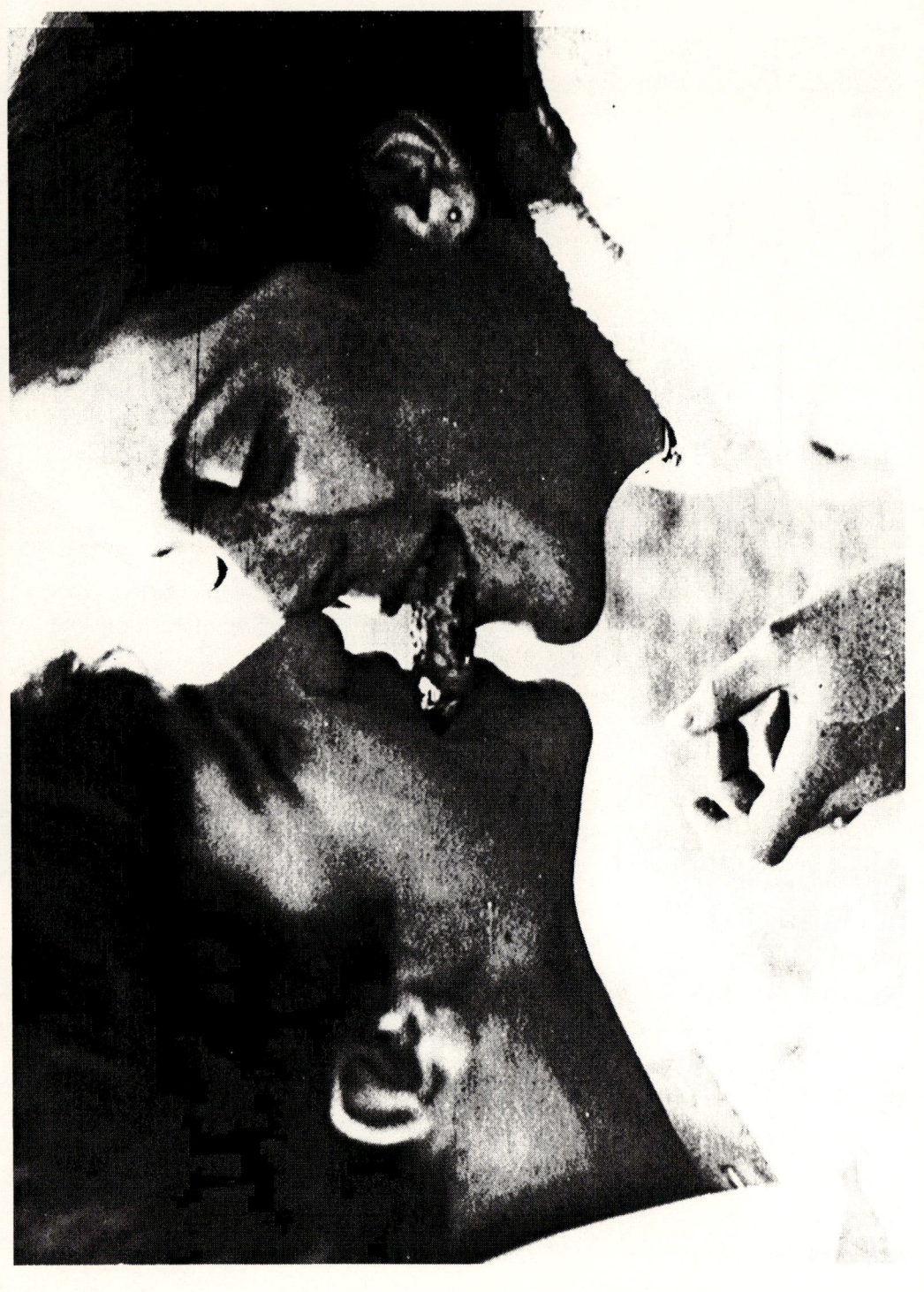

The Groom's Choice Cookies

Beat	4 eggs until very light
Gradually add	
	1 cup honey
Sift &	2 cups flour
Add	2 tsp. soda
	2 tsp. cinnamon
	½ tsp. cardamon
	½ tsp. cloves
Beat well	
Add	1 tsp. grated orange rind
	1 tsp. grated lemon rind
	1 cup currants (wash and soak until plump)
	1 cup chopped almonds

Bake in 2 greased 10x12 pans at 350F for 15-20 minutes. Cut into squares while warm. Ice with simple confectioners' icing.
(5 dozen cookies)

A nice contrast to The Brides Kisses. These should be made ahead of time to mellow in cookie tins. Recipe can easily be doubled.

After School Cookies

Beat	1 egg
Beat in	2/3 cup brown sugar
Stir in	1/3 cup melted margarine
	1 tsp. vanilla
Sift &	1 cup flour
Add	½ tsp. baking powder
	¼ tsp. salt
Add	2/3 cup raisins

Spread in greased 9x9 pan. Sprinkle top with 2 Tbsp. cinnamon and sugar (mixed). Bake at **350F** for 20 minutes. Don't overbake. Leave in pan. Cut into bars.
(2 dozen cookies)

One of the best quick recipes. No creaming. Only 25 minutes from thought to mouth.

Orange Blossom Bars

Beat	2 eggs
Beat in	1 1/3 cups granulated sugar
Stir in	2/3 cup melted margarine
Sift &	2 cups flour
Add	1 tsp. baking powder
	½ tsp. salt
Add &	3 Tbsp. grated orange rind
Stir	6 Tbsp. orange juice

Optional and really **great:**
Add	½ cup diced orange gumdrops or orange jellies

Spread in well greased 9x9 pan. Bake at 350F for 25-30 minutes. Leave in pan. Cut into bars. Can be iced for a dessert. Great as a snack.
(36 bars)

To brighten any day these quick and easy bars are loved by all ages.

Divine Date Balls

Beat	2 eggs until light and creamy
	¾ tsp. salt
	½ tsp. almond extract
Add &	½ cup granulated sugar
Beat	½ cup Karo (light corn syrup)
Add	1 cup finely chopped dates
	1 cup chopped nuts

Fold in ¼ cup sifted flour

Pour into two well greased 8-inch layer cake pans or one 10x16 pan. Bake at 275F for 20-25 minutes. Cut into 1-inch squares while still hot. Shape at once into small balls and roll in dish with ½ cup confectioners' sugar.

(3 dozen cookies)

No shortening. It's the syrup that makes them chewy. Make ahead of time for the Christmas tray. Mails well - keeps well.

Carmel Carmelos

Melt   3/4 cube (6 Tbsp.) margarine in a 1 qt. pan
Add   22 crushed graham crackers (scant 2 cups)
Mix well and press into a greased 10x12 baking dish
Add   1 pkg. (6 oz.) butterscotch chips
                1 cup shredded coconut
                1 cup sliced almonds
Spread 1 can (15 oz.) sweetened condensed milk on top. See that all area is covered. Bake at **350F** for **25-30** minutes. Almonds on top should be delicately brown. Cut and cool in pan for at least 20 minutes.
(4 dozen cookies)

Teenagers enjoy making this recipe. It will become a family favorite.

Pooh's Honey Cakes

Beat	3 eggs
Add	1 cup honey
Continue beating	
Add & Mix	1 cup whole wheat flour
	½ cup rolled oats
	½ cup wheat germ
	¼ tsp. salt
Add	½ cup chopped dates
	½ cup dried figs
	1 cup chopped nuts

Bake in two 9x9 greased pans (spread ¼-inch thick) at 350F for 15-20 minutes. Cut into strips ½-inch wide and 2 inches long. Roll in powdered sugar. Flavor improves when kept in covered container.
(7 dozen cookies)

Good for hibernation. Keeps indefinitely if you hide them. Full of nutrition for snacks.

Cracker Box Date Bars

Beat	3 eggs until lemon colored
Add	1 cup Kleen raw sugar-gradually beating
	1 tsp. vanilla
Stir in	1 small box of graham crackers
	(rolled fine) 32 crackers-2¼ cups
	½ tsp. baking soda
	½ tsp. salt
Add	1 cup chopped dates
	1 cup chopped walnuts

Spread in greased 9x9 pan and bake at 350F for 30-35 minutes. Sprinkle with powdered sugar. Cut when cool.
(3 dozen bars)

No flour—chewy, nutty flavor. Stays fresh and moist in airtight container. **Mails well.**

Zwieback Date Layers

Melt   ½ cup margarine or butter
Mix with   ½ cup brown sugar
           1 pkg. (6 oz.) crushed Zwieback
Pat into a 8x10 greased pan.
Bake until brown at 325F about 10-12 minutes.
Place over crust
           1 cup finely chopped dates
           1 cup finely chopped nuts
Add the following mixture as you would an icing, covering the date-nut layer thoroughly.
Mix   2 beaten egg whites
           ½ tsp. baking powder
&   2 Tbsp. flour (sifted)
Beat   1 tsp. vanilla
           ¼ tsp. salt
           1 cup brown sugar
Bake until golden brown at 350F for 30 minutes. Cut while still warm. Remove later.
(4-5 dozen cookies)

Unusual flavor grows as these are kept in a tin. Mail them. They're delicious.

Mission Fig Bars

Beat	3 eggs and gradually
Add	¾ cup brown sugar
Add	1 cup sifted flour
	¼ tsp. salt
	1½ tsp. baking powder
Beat well	
Add	1 tsp. vanilla
	1½ cups chopped dried figs
	1 cup chopped walnuts

Bake in greased 10x12 pan. Cut into bars while warm. (4 dozen bars)

A California treat with no shortening needed. Keep them or mail them. Um-m-m-good!

Meditation Bread

Cook for 5 minutes	2 cups raisins
	1 cup honey
	¾ cup water
	¼ cup shortening
Let cool	
Sift	1¾ cups flour
	1 tsp. salt
	½ tsp. baking soda
	1 tsp. cinnamon
	1 tsp. nutmeg
	½ tsp. cloves

Add the above to the cooked mixture. Beat well.

Stir in	1 cup chopped dates
	½ cup dried chopped apricots
	½ cup coarsely chopped nuts

Bake in greased 8x10 pan at 325F for 50 minutes. Cool. Cut before completely cool. Substitute Safflower oil or Soy oil for shortening and omit soda and salt for health food enthusiasts. (4 dozen cookies)

No sugar—No eggs. Keeps well—Mails well. Great for the lunch box. Take along on a Retreat.

Pecan Bars

Cream	½ cup margarine
	1 cup brown sugar
	½ tsp. salt
Add	1 cup wheat germ
	½ cup quick oats

Spread mixture in 8x10 greased pan. Bake at 325F for 15 minutes or delicately brown.

Beat	2 eggs until foamy
Add &	1 cup brown sugar
Beat	1 tsp. vanilla
Sift &	2 Tbsp. flour
Add	½ tsp. baking powder
	¼ tsp. salt
Blend in	1 cup diced pecans
	1 cup shredded coconut

Spread above mixture over crust and return to oven (325F) and bake an additional 20 minutes. Cool and cut into rectangles.
(3 dozen bars)

Tastes like Pecan Pie. But better for you. Serve as dessert with ice cream.

Hibernation Cookies

Cream	½ cup margarine
	1 cup sugar
Add	4 eggs one at a time, beat after each
Sift &	4 cups flour
Add	½ tsp. baking soda
	½ tsp. salt

Divide into three parts. If necessary, knead additional flour into dough to make sure it is stiff enough to roll without sticking. Roll the first layer and pat out on a 10x15 jellyroll sheet. Sprinkle with mixture of 2 Tbsp. cinnamon and ¼ cup sugar. Spread on filling and repeat with second layer of dough, cinnamon and sugar, and filling. Finish with third layer of dough. Cut in diamond patterns before baking. Bake 1 hour at 325F. Filling: 1 cup Muesli (also known as Familia or Swissi); 1 cup date sugar; 1 cup raisins; 1 cup favorite jam; 1 tsp. lemon juice. These ingredients may be changed to suit your tastes.
(100 pieces)

Do your baking in advance of your needs. Keep in tins for a party or friends who drop in.

Cake n' Candy Cookies

Layer 1

Cream	1 cup margarine
	1 cup brown sugar
Beat &	1 egg
Stir in	½ tsp. vanilla
Sift &	2 cups flour
Stir in	½ tsp. baking powder
	½ tsp. salt

Spread in greased 10x15 shallow jellyroll pan. Bake at 350F for 20 minutes. Cool in pan.

Layer 2

Make a butter frosting by placing ½ cup soft margarine, 1/3 cup light cream and 1 cup sugar in pan, cooking and stirring occasionally until soft ball stage. Beat until creamy and spread over first layer.

Layer 3

Melt over hot water 2 pkgs. (6 oz.) semi-sweet chocolate bits. Spread over frosting and sprinkle with ½ to 1 cup chopped nuts. Put in refrigerator and after 10 minutes cut into squares.
(6-7 dozen cookies)

The cookie that has everything. Three layers of delightful flavor. Not recommended for the dieter.

Happy Holiday Bars

Cream   ½ cup butter or margarine
            ½ cup sifted powdered sugar
Add   2 egg yolks, one at a time beating after each addition
Mix in   1 cup sifted flour

Press into 8x10 pan. Bake at **350F** for **10-12 minutes**. Whip ½ to ¾ cup red currant jelly (or jelly of your choice). Spread over hot cookie layer. Beat 2 egg whites until stiff, gradually beating in 2 tsp. sugar and cinnamon. Fold in 1 cup chopped filberts. Spread over jelly layer. Bake at **350F** for **20 minutes** more. Cool slightly. Cut in bars.
(3-4 dozen bars)

The red currant jelly make these pretty for celebrations. May be varied to your taste.

Open Sesames

Beat	3 eggs
Mix in	1 cup honey
Sift &	2 cups flour
Add	1 tsp. baking powder
	1 cup chopped dates
	1 cup chopped figs
	1 tsp. almond extract

Spread in jellyroll pan so that batter is ½-inch thick. Sprinkle ½-cup (a 2 1/8-oz. pkg.) toasted sesame seeds.* Bake at 350F for 15-20 minutes. Cut into strips ½"x2". Sprinkle with powdered sugar. Keep in a tin and the flavor improves. *·Prepare by putting sesame seeds on aluminum foil on baking sheet in 350F oven for about 15 minutes.
(5 dozen)

Honey, dates, and sesame seeds make these no-shortening bars easy to keep and mail.

Armenian Cookies (Abajian's)

Mix   1½ cups drawn butter
(Takes about 2 cups of melted butter. Sediment can be used to flavor vegetables.
         ¾ cup granulated sugar
Mix in   3 egg yolks, beating after each addition
         3 cups sifted flour, one cup at a time
Flatten into a jellyroll pan. Brush well with beaten egg whites. Cut into diamonds and put a blanched slivered almond on each diamond shape. Bake at 350F for 15-20 minutes. Cut again after baking and cool in pan.
(About 100 cookies)

Skish Kabob and Armenian Cookies go great together. The secret is the drawn butter.

Your Favorite Jam Bars

Mix   1½ cups sifted whole wheat flour
              1 tsp. baking powder
              1 cup brown sugar
              1½ cups Roman Meal Cereal (contains four grains)
Cut in   ¾ cup butter or margarine until crumbly

Pat 2/3 of this mixture into 8x12 pan. Spread with 1 cup apricot, boysenberry, raspberry or whatever jam you like. Cover with remaining crumb mixture. Bake at 350F about 35 minutes or until crusty on top. Cool and cut into bars.

Variation:
   One to two cups of mincemeat may be used in place of jam.
(4 dozen bars)

This can be as much you as the kinds of jam you prefer. It's eggless and quick. Packs well and mails well.

Prune Pickups

Beat	3 egg whites
	¼ tsp. salt
Gradually add &	
Beat in	¾ cup Kleen raw sugar
	(brown may be substituted)
Blend in	3 egg yolks
	¼ cup sugar
	1 Tbsp. lemon juice
	1 tsp. grated lemon rind

Fold this mixture into beaten egg whites

Fold in	1 cup sifted whole wheat flour
Fold in	¾ cup pitted chopped prunes
	1 cup chopped walnuts (filberts are good too)

Bake in 9x9 greased pan at 325F for 30-40 minutes. Cut into bars and roll in powdered sugar while still warm.
(3 dozen bars)

Mails well—Packs well. Good in lunch boxes. No shortening—quick mixing.

Rolled Cookies

These cookies can be the most creative and the most fun of all. Since you do them in two steps they can be mixed and then rolled out at a later baking time. Rolled cookies are mainly varied by different shapes, designs, frosting, and decorating, and a few basic doughs are sufficient for numerous different cookies.

Method: Mix the dough as you would drop cookies unless otherwise directed. There is more flour since the dough must be stiffer in order to roll properly. Chilling is often best and when you decide to bake, take out a small amount at a time. Roll on a lightly floured board using as little flour as possible. Try to keep from rerolling dough as this tends to make them tough. Dip the cutter into flour for ease of imprint.

If you do not have the desired cutter or are making something like the cookie Christmas tree, make a cardboard design and after rolling the dough, place the cardboard pattern on the dough and cut around with a sharp knife. Children can help with the cutting and decorating. The rolled cookie is an important basis for the filled and sandwich cookie and many of the traditional European recipes.

The Sugar Cookie Times Six-

Just to get you started on some variations, the Sugar Cookie can be changed from within or without. Here are some of the most popular cookies which can be made by making only a change or two.

Butterscotch Cookies - substitute brown sugar for granulated sugar. Orange Rolled Cookies - omit vanilla and add 1 tsp. orange juice and 2 tsp. grated orange rind. Spice Cookies - sift 1 tsp. cinnamon, ½ tsp. allspice, ¼ tsp. cloves, ½ tsp. ginger and add with sifted dry ingredients. Chocolate Crisps - add 2 heaping Tbsp. cocoa to sifted dry ingredients. Nutty Wafers - add 1 cup finely chopped nuts to dough. Raisin Rollers - add 1 cup chopped raisins to dough.

Rolled Sugar Cookie

Cream	½ cup butter
	¾ cup sugar
Add	1 beaten egg
	2 Tbsp. milk
	1 tsp. vanilla
Sift &	2 cups flour
Stir in	1 tsp. baking powder
	¼ tsp. salt

Beat well and if necessary, add more flour, a little at a time, to make stiffer dough. Wrap in wax paper and refrigerate. Later roll out on floured board to thickness of 1/8-inch. Cut in desired shapes. Place on lightly greased sheet and bake at 375F for 10 minutes. Watch carefully. Use wide spatula to place on cookie sheet and to remove.

(4 dozen cookies)

This recipe can be doubled very easily. Then cut them out in various shapes and sizes. Let the children decorate with candy, nuts, rasins, etc. Lots of fun for them on a rainy day. Try all of the variations.

The Sugar Cookie Dresses Up

1. Brush cut cookies with egg white and sprinkle with chopped almonds. 2. Color one part of the dough with food coloring. Roll one part 1/8-inch thick. Then roll the other part 1/8-inch thick and put the two together lightly and roll as for jellyroll. Chill and cut into slices. Bake. 3. Cut cookies. Bake. Cover with icing, tinted or plain. 4. Cut cookies. Decorate with colored candies or colored sugar. Bake. 5. Cut cookies into Christmas shapes. Outline with decorators frosting. If the cookies are to be hung on a tree, make a small hole near the top and insert a dried bean to keep hole from closing during baking. 6. Cut. Decorate with gumdrop slices. Bake until cookie is lightly brown and gumdrops melted.

Paper Dollies

Cream	1 cup butter
	½ cup honey
	2 egg yolks, slightly beaten
	1 Tbsp. grated lemon rind
Sift &	4 cups flour
Add	¾ tsp. baking powder
Add	1 Tbsp. lemon juice

Chill dough in two parts. Use as needed. Roll out and cut into shapes of boys and girls. Bake at 350F 10-15 minutes. Bake one inch apart on greased baking sheet.
(8-10 dozen cookies)

A soft shaped cookie to please Christmas appetites. Children can help decorate. Use your imagination and cut your shapes from cardboard.

Lemon Loverlies

Cream	1 cup butter
	2 cups granulated sugar
Add	3 beaten egg yolks
	3 Tbsp. lemon juice
	1 tsp. lemon rind
Sift &	2¼ cups flour
Add	¼ tsp. salt

Mix thoroughly and chill for at least 3 hours. Roll out on greased sheet. Bake at 375F for 12-15 minutes. Brush tops with egg white and sprinkle with a little sugar or brush each cookie with cold water for a cracked surface.

(3 dozen cookies)

A tart satisfying treat for any age.

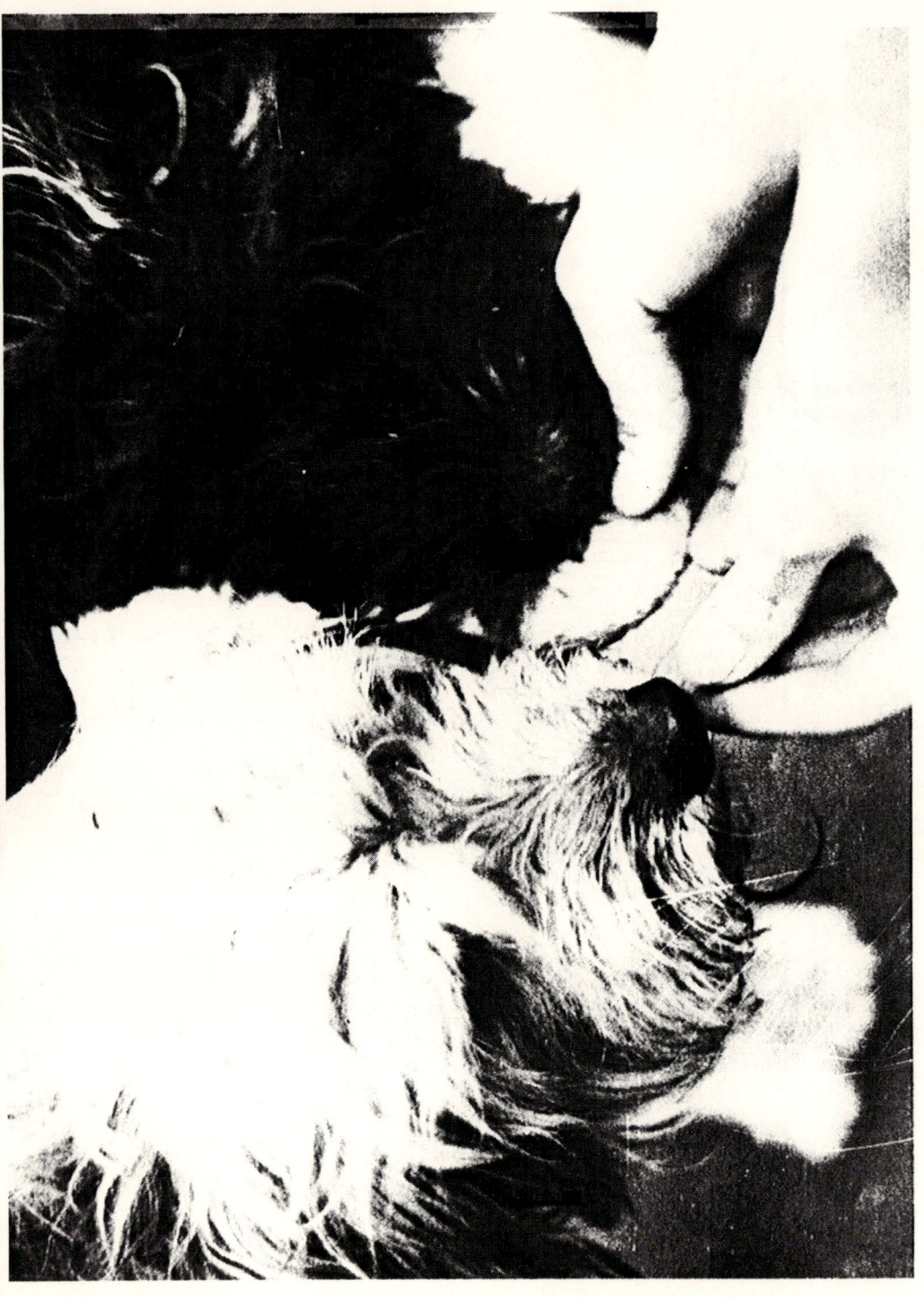

Scotch Shortbread

Cream	1 cup butter (no substitutions)
	½ cup granulated sugar
Sift &	2 cups flour
Add	½ cup cornstarch

Mix well with hands about ten minutes and knead into dough.
Roll out and cut into cakes about 1/3-inch thick. Cakes should be at least three inches in diameter. Prick the center with a fork in a design and score into quarters. Put shortbread on brown paper placed on a baking sheet. Bake at 300F for 30-45 minutes for the smaller size. Watch at intervals. Cakes should be delicately brown. Double the recipe and make cakes same thickness but larger in diameter. Keep in a tin afterwards. Make size according to tin for storing or gift giving.
(2 dozen - 3 inch diameter size)

This old Scottish recipe makes a wonderful gift. Please pay careful attention to the technique described. The results are worth the extra effort.

Cream Cheese Cut Outs

Cream	½ cup butter
	3 ounces cream cheese (softened)
	2 Tbsp. granulated sugar
Add	½ tsp. vanilla
Sift &	1½ cups flour
Add	¼ tsp. salt

Mix well. Chill. Roll out 1/8- to 1/4-inch thick. Cut into fancy shapes. Place on lightly greased cookie sheet and sprinkle with cinnamon sugar or colored sugar as desired. Bake at 350F for 10-12 minutes.

(3 dozen cookies)

A distinctive flavor is achieved, delicate but not too sweet, by using cream cheese.

Peanut Pinwheels

Cream	½ cup margarine
	1 cup brown sugar
Beat in	1 egg
	½ cup soft peanut butter
	2 Tbsp. milk
Sift &	1 cup 2 Tbsp. flour
Stir in	½ tsp. salt
	½ tsp. baking powder

Mix dough and roll in an 8x14 inch rectangle on a piece of paper. Melt one 8 oz. semisweet chocolate bar in aluminum foil and cool. Spread over dough. Roll as for a jellyroll. Chill at least an hour. Slice off as needed and place on ungreased cookie sheet. Bake at 350F for 8-10 minutes.
(3 dozen cookies)

Add variety to the cookie tray. This recipe is a favorite with children so make it for the next Cub Scout meeting.

Orgy Makers

Work into	½ pound butter
A dough	2 cups 2 Tbsp. flour
	½ cup vanilla sugar
	2 egg yolks

Roll approximately 1/8- to 1/4-inch thick. Cut into shapes. Brush with egg white. Bake at 325F for 8-10 minutes or until light brown. Put together in pairs with apricot jam.
(2 dozen cookies)

Try boysenberry, cherry, strawberry, or grape jam or use your family's favorite preserve and watch their delight as they bite into these.

Pioneer Gingersnaps

Cream	½ cup shortening
	¾ cup Kleen raw sugar
Add	1 egg
	½ cup molasses

Dissolve 2 tsp. baking soda in 2 tsp. hot water and add to above mixture

Sift &	2½ cups stone ground whole wheat flour
Add	½ tsp. cinnamon
	1 tsp. ginger
	¼ tsp. salt

Chill. Roll on lightly floured board and cut 1/8-inch thick with round cookie cutter. Place on greased baking sheet. Bake at 350F for 10-12 minutes. For a crinkled surface brush each cookie with water before baking.
(6 dozen 2" cookies)

This spicy cookie really snaps. Try serving it with milk or lemonade the next time the neighbors gather at your home.

Honey-Holly Wreaths

Heat with   ½ cup honey
Care   ½ cup shortening
When cool add sifted dry ingredients.
    2 cups flour
    1 tsp. cinnamon
    1 tsp. lemon rind
    ½ tsp. cardamon
    ½ tsp. nutmeg
    1 tsp. baking soda

Roll out to ¼-inch thickness and cut with round cutter with a hole in center. Bake on greased cookie sheet at 350F for 12-15 minutes. When cool, frost with white icing and pipe in green. Decorate with red cinnamon candies to look like holly wreath.
(4 dozen cookies)

Try decorating for the Holidays or serve them plain for everyday eating enjoyment. No eggs are required and they keep well in your cookie tin or jar.

Running Gingerbread Men

Combine & Mix	½ cup brown sugar
	½ cup shortening
	1 egg
	¾ cup molasses
	1 tsp. baking soda
	1 tsp. cinnamon
	1 tsp. cloves
	1 tsp. salt
	2 tsp. ginger
	2 tsp. lemon juice
Add	3 cups sifted flour
	(If necessary add more to make stiff dough.)

Mix well. Wrap and chill overnight. Roll out as needed and cut in gingerbreadman shapes. Put raisins for eyes, red hots for nose and mouth, and candies for buttons. Place on lightly greased sheet and bake at 375F for 6-8 minutes. After cool they can be outlined with decorators icing. The quantity will vary with the size of the gingerbreadmen. I have four different cutters. One big man is fun for a special child. It is nice to make a batch of smaller ones for all the children in the neighborhood.
(3 dozen 3"x2" size cookies)

Our family gift to the neighborhood children. You can cut out lions, bunnies, or Teddy bears.

Fruit Filled Cookies - Fig Newtons

Cream	1 cup honey
	1 cup shortening
	1 cup brown sugar
Add	2 eggs
	½ lemon rind and juice
Sift &	6 cups of flour (whole wheat flour may be used)
Add	2 tsp. baking powder
	1 tsp. salt
	1 tsp. baking soda

Mix thoroughly and chill. Roll dough quite thin in strips of desired size. Five inches by three inches is a good size. Put filling in center and fold over. Press down with fork around edges to seal. Bake at 400F for 15 minutes.

(4 dozen cookies)

Make several kinds with one batch: fig, raisin, date, prune, or pineapple.

Fruit Fillings

Fig Filling:

Combine &	4 cups chopped figs
Cook	1 cup honey
15 minutes	¼ cup water
Always	3 Tbsp. lemon juice
Stirring	3 Tbsp. orange juice
	(Cool)

Many-Fruited Filling:

Combine &	½ cup chopped raisins
Cook	½ cup chopped figs
Slowly	½ cup chopped dates
Until thick	½ cup chopped walnuts
(10-15 minutes)	½ cup sugar
	½ cup water
	2 Tbsp. lemon juice
	2 Tbsp. orange juice
	(Cool)

Pineapple Filling:

Combine &	1 cup honey
Cook	4 Tbsp. cornstarch
Stirring	1¼ cups crushed, drained pineapple
Constantly	¾ cup pineapple juice
	4 Tbsp. lemon juice
	(Cool)

Mincemeat

Canned or homemade may be used as a filling. Be sure that it is thick enough. You may have to cook it "down".

Celebration Cookies

Cream	1 cup butter or margarine
	1¾ cups granulated sugar
Add	2 well beaten eggs
	2 tsp. vanilla
	4 Tbsp. Brandy
Sift &	3 cups flour
Add	3 tsp. baking powder
	½ tsp. salt
Add	½ cup finely chopped almonds

If necessary add more sifted flour, a little at a time up to ½ cup, to make dough stiffer. Chill at least 4 hours. Roll out 1/8-inch thick and cut into fancy shapes; i.e., crecents, stars, etc. Bake at 375F for 10 minutes. Frost with a chocolate frosting is desired for added delight.
(6 dozen cookies)

A special cookie to please and surprise. Great for holidays.

Vibration Cookies

Mix &	1 cup natural honey
Boil	½ cup molasses (unsulfured with no preservatives)
Allow to cool	
Stir in	1 cup date sugar
	1 tsp. grated lemon rind
	1 Tbsp. lemon juice
Sift &	2 cups stone ground wheat flour
Stir in	1 cup Granola (Muesli if not available)
	1 tsp. cinnamon
	1 tsp. ground cloves
	½ tsp. cardamom

Mix and form into two rolls and wrap in aluminum foil. Chill in refrigerator. Slice ¼-inch thick and roll 1/8-inch flat with rolling pin. Makes long oval cookie. If greater yield is desired cut the size in half. Place on greased baking sheet and bake at 350F for 8-10 minutes. Increase baking time if you enjoy a more crunchy, brittle cookie.
(4-6 dozen cookies)

This recipe was created for the person who appreciates natural nutrition. It contains no eggs, sugar, or leavening and therefore will keep indefinitely.

Walnut Torte Cookies

Cream	½ cup soft butter (no substitutes)
	1/3 cup granulated sugar
Add	1 cup sifted flour
	2/3 cups ground walnuts

Chill at least 4 hours or overnight. Roll out and cut into 1½-inch rounds about 1/8-inch thick. Lift onto ungreased sheet with wide spatula. Bake at 375F for 8-10 minutes. Place a spoonful of frosting on a cookie and top with another cookie, making a sandwich. Frost sandwich with same frosting and top with a walnut half. Cocoa Satin Frosting: Cream 2 Tbsp. butter with 1 cup confectioners' sugar and 2 Tbsp. powdered cocoa.
(2 dozen cookies)

A specialty to make you famous. The ground walnuts add the unusual flavor.

Kindness Cookies

Beat	3 eggs
Add	1 cup honey
Continue beating	
Add & Mix	1 cup stone ground whole wheat flour
	½ cup wheat germ
	½ cup Instant Roman Meal Cereal
	¼ tsp. salt
Add	½ cup black mission figs (chopped)
	½ cup raisins
	½ cup chopped filberts (hazelnuts)

Roll between waxpaper to 1/8-inch thickness, cut with cookie cutter and bake at 350F for 10-12 minutes.
(6 dozen cookies)

No sugar and lots of fruit make up this recipe created expressly for you to give to your love.

Penny Wise Cookies

Heat carefully until melted
       ½ cup honey
       ½ cup vegetable shortening
When cool add
       2 cups sifted flour
       ½ tsp. cinnamon
       ½ tsp. cloves (or spice you wish)
       1 tsp. baking soda
Mix and beat. Form into dough. Roll out to ¼-inch thickness and cut into desired shapes with cookie cutter. Bake on greased cookie sheet at 350F for 12-15 minutes. For special occasions decorate with small candies before baking or frost when cool.
(4 dozen cookies)

An everyday cookie that can be made fancy with your own ideas. Because the ingredients are staples, these are easy to assemble.

Pressed Cookies

These cookies are made by forcing the dough through a pastry tube or cookie press thus making different shapes. Follow the directions of your particular press. The dough is very rich and mixed as for drop cookies using soft butter. The dough should be chilled to keep from spreading, but it crumbles if too cold.

Bake until cookies are set but not brown. Dough for pressed cookies can be rolled out or you can form the cookies into a ball and press down with a glass if you do not have the cookie press and want to try the recipes. However, the rosettes, fluted bars, molded stars and shapes found in the press set make it a very festive and party cookie. The dough may be tinted and cookies decorated.

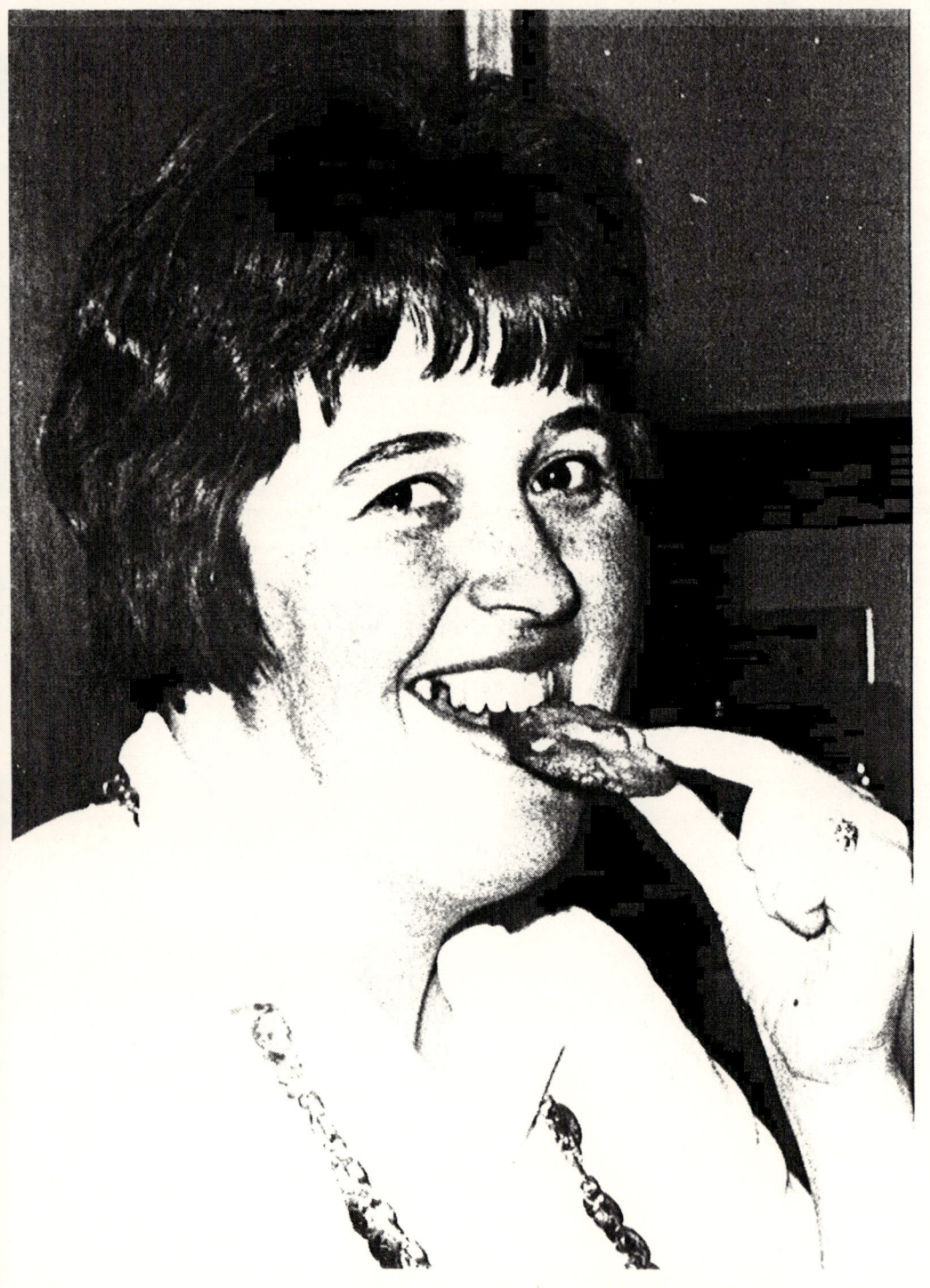

Vanilla Spritz

Cream	¾ cup butter (no substitutes)
	½ cup vanilla sugar
Add	1 egg yolk
	1 tsp. vanilla
Sift &	2 cups cake flour
Add	½ tsp. salt

Mix well into a smooth dough and force through a cookie press. Follow directions on your cookie press. If dough is too soft refrigerate until firm. Bake at 375F for 7-10 minutes.

Chocolate Spritz: Add 2 squares of melted unsweetened chocolate to the shortening. Spicy Spritz: Sift ½ tsp. cinnamon, ¼ tsp. nutmeg, ¼ tsp. cloves, and add to dry ingredients.
(3 dozen cookies)

Spritz means "spurted out". Try all sorts of variations and shapes. It's fun.

Very Almond Spritz

Mix Together	½ cup butter
	1/3 cup granulated sugar
	2 egg yolks
	1 tsp. almond flavoring
Work in by hand	½ cup ground almonds
	¾ cup sifted flour

Force dough through a cookie press onto ungreased sheet. Brush with eggwhite and sprinkle with mixture of ¼ cup finely chopped almonds and sugar. Bake at 400F from 6-8 minutes depending on size.
(3 dozen cookies)

Ground almonds make the delicate difference. If you have no cookie press, form them into 1-inch balls and press flat with a glass tumbler.

Feather Flakes

Cream	1 cup butter or margarine
	1 3 oz. pkg. cream cheese
	1 cup granulated sugar
Add &	1 egg yolk
Beat	1 tsp. vanilla
	1 tsp. grated orange peel (or 1 tsp. lemon peel)
Sift &	2½ cups cake flour
Add	½ tsp. salt
	¼ tsp. cinnamon

Form into dough and force through press onto ungreased sheet. Decorate with chocolate sprinkles, tiny candies or chopped nuts. Bake at 350F for 12-15 minutes. Remove at once and cool. (6-7 dozen cookies)

Rich, light and pretty. Change from orange to lemon as you please.

Ginger Snips

Cream	¾ cup shortening
	¾ cup brown sugar
	¾ cup molasses
	1 egg
Mix well	
Sift &	3 cups flour
Add	½ tsp. salt
	1½ tsp. baking soda
	½ tsp. ground cloves
	1 tsp. cinnamon
	1 tsp. ginger

Mix thoroughly and force through cookie press. Sprinkle with sugar. Bake at 375F for 12-15 minutes. Ice with Butter-Sugar frosting, colored orange. Add 1 tsp. grated orange peel.
(6 dozen cookies)

These spicy snips are the answer for your Halloween treats. They smell and taste like autumn.

Parmesan Sticks

Cream	½ cup butter (no substitutes)
	1 cup grated Parmesan cheese
Sift &	1 cup flour
Add	½ tsp. baking powder
Add	3 Tbsp. cold water
Mix well	

Fill cookie press half full. Form sticks on ungreased cookie sheet by using suitable plate. At this point you can put in refrigerator or freezer to pop out just before serving. Bake at 375F for 8-10 minutes.

(3 dozen cookies)

Form these flaky appetizers ahead of your party and put them in your freezer until the big event arrives. Add herbs to your taste.

Sour Cream Bars

Cream	1 cup butter or margarine
	1 cup granulated sugar
Add	2 egg yolks
	½ cup sour cream
Beat	1 tsp. vanilla
Sift	4 cups flour
	½ tsp. salt
	1 tsp. nutmeg
	½ tsp. baking soda

Add the above gradually, mixing well after each addition. Force dough through press with desired forms. Bake at 375F for 10 minutes, depending upon size of cookie.
(8-10 dozen cookies)

A large recipe that pleases everyone. Use the bar shape or vary with the other fancy forms from your cookie press.

Peanut Butter Spritz

Mix Together	1 cup shortening
	1 cup peanut butter
	1 cup sugar
	1 cup brown sugar
	2 eggs
Sift & Add	2½ cups flour
	1 tsp. baking powder
	2 tsp. soda
	½ tsp. salt
Add	2 cups crushed peanuts

Force dough through press onto ungreased sheet. Bake at $375°$ from 8-10 minutes. Frost with chocolate icing for variation.
(10 dozen cookies)

These crunchy cookies are the favorite of many small cookie lovers.

El Camino Orange Drops

Cream	1 cup shortening
	1 cup brown sugar
Add	1 Tbsp. orange juice
Add	1 beaten egg
	1 tsp. grated orange rind
Sift &	2½ cups rice flour
Add	½ tsp. salt
	¼ tsp. soda

Add sifted ingredients to creamed mixture a little at a time.
Fill cookie press half full. Press out desired shapes on ungreased cookie sheet. If you have no press, form into a ball and flatten with a glass. Bake at 375F for 10-12 minutes. When cool frost with simple confectioners' icing made with orange juice. Garnish with half date.
(6 dozen cookies)

These refreshingly different cookies combine orange and rice flour. Excellent for Halloween or Thanksgiving. Tint icing if desired.

Refrigerator Cookies

This cookie dough is rich with butter and sugar and stiff because of the quantity of flour. Recipes are usually for a large amount and are divided into three or four rolls 1½ inchs in diameter. These are wrapped in waxed paper and chilled at least 4 hours or overnight in the refrigerator. This process may be speeded by putting in the freezer for an hour or they may be stored in the freezer for many months.

Method: Cream, beat, and add ingredients as for drop cookies but mold into rolls. After chilling, cookies are sliced thin (1/8- to 1/4-inch) and baked on an ungreased sheet quickly. When slicing cookies use a sharp knife with a sawing motion and no pressure. The knife should be wiped often. These cookies are particularly useful because they can be mixed ahead of time and then baked fresh when needed.

Rescue Cookies

Cream	1 cup butter or margarine
	1 cup granulated sugar
	1 cup brown sugar
Add	3 eggs one at a time
	1½ tsp. vanilla

Beat and mix well

Sift	3 cups flour
&	1 tsp. salt
Add	1 tsp. soda
Add	½ to 1 cup of additional sifted flour

Roll in three parts. Wrap and refrigerate. Slice 1/8- to 1/4-inch and place on ungreased baking sheet. Bake 6-8 minutes.

Variations:

Add 2 to 3 tsp. cinnamon or other spices to the sifted dry ingredients. Add ½ cup very finely chopped nuts after flour addition. Add 3 squares of melted unsweetened chocolate to the butter and sugar mixture. Just about any variation already included will work with these.

(6-8 dozen cookies)

This Make Now, Bake Later Cookie is the complete and classic cookie. Always keep some on hand.

Chocolate Spiral Cookies

Use the recipe for Basic Refrigerator Cookies or your own favorite refrigerator cookie recipe. However, before adding the flour divide the batter in half. Keep one half plain and add half of sifted dry ingredients. Add 2 squares of melted unsweetened chocolate to the other half and then add the remaining half of the sifted dry ingredients. Roll each part of dough about 1/8-inch thick on lightly floured wax paper. Plain strip should be ½-inch longer than chocolate strip. Place chocolate strip on top of plain strip and roll. Wrap in waxed paper and chill overnight. Slice thinly and bake according to recipe directions.

An eye pleasing variation for special occasions.

Chocolate Chippies

Cream	1 cup margarine
	½ cup granulated sugar
	½ cup brown sugar
Add	1 egg
	2 Tbsp. orange juice
	1 Tbsp. grated orange rind
Mix well	
Sift &	2½ cups flour
Stir	¼ tsp. baking soda
	¼ tsp. salt
Add	6 oz. semi-sweet chocolate bar grated

Shape and chill. Slice thin. Bake on ungreased sheet at 375F for 10-12 minutes. If you wish to omit the orange flavor add 1 tsp. vanilla and 2 Tbsp. water. Finely chopped nuts may also be added. (6 dozen cookies)

An ever ready chocolate chip cookie. Ready for every occasion.

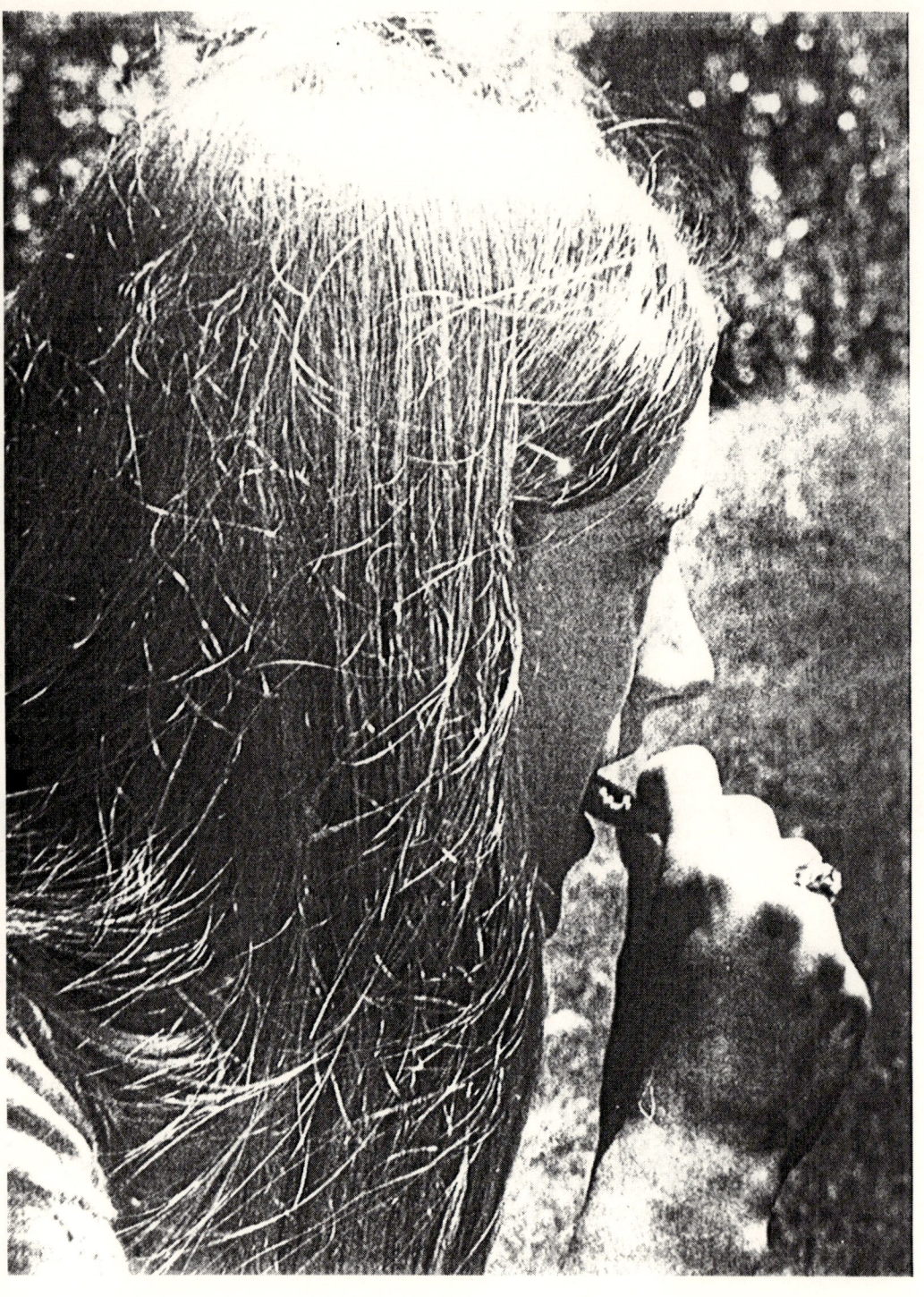

Maple-Nut Marvels

Cream	½ cup shortening
	1 cup brown sugar
Add	1 egg
	½ tsp. maple flavoring
Sift &	1½ cups flour
Add	1½ tsp. baking powder
	¼ tsp. salt

Shape in roll and chill at least 4 hours. Slice and sprinkle tops with ¼ cup chopped English walnuts. Bake at 350F for 8-10 minutes. Remove at once.
(4 dozen cookies)

A distinctive maple-nut flavor. Serve with vanilla ice cream or pudding. It will become one of your favorites.

Gumdrop Slices

Cream	1 cup butter or margarine
	1½ cups sifted confectioners sugar
	1 tsp. vanilla
Beat in	1 egg
Sift &	2½ cups flour
Stir	1 tsp. soda
	1 tsp. cream of tartar
	¼ tsp. salt
Mix well	
Add	1 cup small gumdrops sliced

Shape dough into two rolls and refrigerate. Slice and bake at 375F about 10-12 minutes. Cool before removing from pan. (6 dozen cookies)

A favorite with children. Wonderful for parties and Christmas. Use your favorite colors.

Allen's All Americans - Oatmeal Cookies

Cream	1 cup margarine
	1 cup brown sugar
	1 cup granulated sugar
Add	2 eggs slightly beaten
	1 tsp. vanilla
Mix well	
Add	1½ cups whole wheat flour
	1 tsp. baking soda
	1 tsp. salt
Mix well	
Add	3 cups Quick Oats

Divide into three parts. Add ½ cup finely chopped nuts to one part. Add finely chopped raisins and dates to another part and keep one part plain. Chill until hard. Slice and bake at 400F for 10 minutes.
(6 dozen cookies)

This recipe yields enough for the entire team. Divide the dough into three parts, adding nuts to one, raisins or dates to another, and leave the last plain. You will please everyone.

Cinnamon Circles

Cream	1/3 cup butter
	1/3 cup granulated sugar
	1 tsp. grated lemon rind
Add	2 egg yolks
	2/3 cup ground almonds
Beat well	
Sift &	1 cup flour
Add	¼ tsp. salt
	1½ tsp. cinnamon

Blend in gradually and mix thoroughly. Use hands for smoothness. Shape into roll and refrigerate at least 4 hours. Cut into ¼-inch slices. Brush with egg white and sprinkle with cinnamon sugar or frost after baking with chocolate frosting if desired. Bake at 375F for 10-12 minutes.
(2-3 dozen cookies)

This unusual ground almond recipe will decorate your tea tray beautifully.

Mincemeat Miracles

Cream   ¾ cup shortening
             1 cup brown sugar
Add   1 tsp. vanilla
             1 tsp. grated lemon peel
             1 egg
Mix well
Sift   2½ cups flour
             ½ tsp. salt
             ½ tsp. baking soda
             1 tsp. cinnamon

Add the above mixture alternately with ½ cup mincemeat and ½ cup chopped walnuts. Shape and chill. Slice ¼-inch thick. Bake on ungreased cookie sheet at 350F for 15 minutes.
(4 dozen cookies)

So quick and easy to prepare and bake, you will enjoy making these often.

Wilshire Tea Time Cookies

Cream	½ cup butter (no substitutes)
	3 Tbsp. cocoa
	6 Tbsp. vanilla sugar*
Add	1 cup sifted flour
	1 cup ground walnuts
	2 egg yolks

Work into a smooth dough first with a wooden spoon and then with fingers. Roll into two rolls and refrigerate at least 4 hours. Cut into thin slices and place on ungreased cookie sheet. Bake at 325F for 10 minutes. When cool ice with vanilla icing and sprinkle with finely chopped walnuts or pistachios. Cookies may be iced with chocolate or mocha icing also. * Sugar in which a vanilla bean has been stored.
(4 dozen cookies)

For that very special occasion, this cookie will do the trick and yet there is nothing tricky to the recipe. The ground nuts make the difference.

Barbary Coast Cookies

Cream	¾ cup butter or margarine
	1 cup brown sugar
Add	2 eggs beaten
	1 tsp. dark rum (or rum extract)
Beat thoroughly	
Sift &	2 cups flour
Stir in	2 Tbsp. instant coffee
	½ tsp. baking soda
	½ tsp. baking powder
	½ tsp. salt.

Blend. Shape into 2 rolls about 1½-inch in diameter. Chill. Slice thin and place on ungreased cookie sheet. Place a pecan half on top of each cookie. Bake at 375F for 8-10 minutes.
(6 dozen cookies)

Golden nuggets from old San Francisco's Barbary Coast with a delicate rum-coffee flavor.

Et Cetera Cookies

Just to prove there are always exceptions to categories and descriptions, this is where you find the different cookies that may not be sweet, baked, or beaten but are made to be eaten.

Use cake and cookie mixes but don't miss the fun. Put a little of your own mystique in it. Always add something even if it's your own thumb print and a droplet of jam.

Berry Yous

Combine   1 16 oz. package of cookie mix
               ½ cup sifted flour
               ¼ cup water (room temperature)

Work until well blended. Chill 15 minutes. Shape into 1-inch balls. Roll in slightly beaten egg white. Then roll in ½ cup finely chopped almonds. Bake at 350F on ungreased cookie sheet for 25 minutes. Remove from sheet and make an indentation with your thumb. Fill the indentation with a berry preserve of your choice. (3 dozen cookies)

Easy mixing and fun making. Use your favorite berry preserve and let the children spoon it in.

Brownie Spoonfuls

Mix   1 16 oz. package of Brownie mix
               1 egg
               ¼ cup vegetable oil
Add   1 cup chopped walnuts

Chill two to three hours. Drop dough by spoonful in confectioners' sugar. Roll into balls. Place on greased baking sheet. Bake at 350F for 10 minutes. Don't overbake.

(3 dozen cookies)

If you can use a spoon you can make these. Use a variety of nuts. Watch carefully while baking.

Little Angels

Mix 1 package of Marble Cake mix
(leave out marbling mix)
1 egg
¼ cup vegetable oil
2 Tbsp. water

Roll out all but ¼ cup. Cut into round faces of desired size. Blend marbling mix with 1 Tbsp. water. Add the ¼ cup dough. Roll out and attach to face for hair. Bake at 375F on lightly greased sheet for 8-10 minutes. You can make eyes and mouth before baking with currants and candies or decorate afterwards with decorators' icing and a toothpick. Be sure to make big smiles unless you want a few devils and Grunchs.
(2-3 dozen depending on size of face)

Serve at Cub Scout Meetings or great for the Sunday School Picnic. Even the Office will like them.

Zippity Zoos

1 small package of vanilla wafers
1 box of animal cookies or iced animals
1 batch of quick frosting as follows:
Add   a small amount of cream to 1 cup
            of sifted confectioners' sugar
Add   dash of salt and
            ½ tsp. vanilla
Blend
Put wafers together with frosting. Add a dab of frosting to top and stand your child's favorite animal on top. Make some for yourself too.

This is a quick treat the older children can prepare for the toddlers.

Glamouroos

1 package of vanilla wafers (size depends upon your wishes)
1 jar of strawberry jam (can be varied)
1 package of pink peppermint patties
½ package of semisweet chocolate bits
Make sandwiches of wafers with jam in between. Put a little jam on bottom of pattie and put on top of wafer. Place a chocolate bit on top. Heat on ungreased cookie sheet at 350F for about 2 to 3 minutes. Cool thoroughly.

The variations for this colorful treat are endless. After you have put your imagination to work, pack them in a pretty glass jar for a gift to that favorite person.

More Instant Cookies

Beat &	½ cup soft peanut butter
Mix	1 can sweetened condensed milk (15-oz.)
Add	2 cups crushed corn flakes
	(raisin bran flakes are good too)
	1 cup long shredded coconut

Drop onto well greased baking sheet. Aluminum foil on baking sheet is fine. Bake at 375F for 10 minutes or until golden. Remove from pan at once.
(4 dozen cookies)

Only 15 minutes to prepare something? No flour, no sifting, no creaming, no chopping; and the best part is you have all the ingredients on your pantry shelf. Try them!

Nob Hill Cookies

Melt   1 6 oz. package of chocolate bits
               (your choice of chocolate)
Add   1 can (15 oz.) Chinese noodles
Mix thoroughly
Drop onto wax paper on a cookie sheet and put into the refrigerator until hard.
Variation:
   Add 1 Tbsp. Creme de Menthe or use minted chocolate bits if desired.
(2 dozen cookies)

Here is another quickie that is rich and elegant - almost like candy.

Brandy Balls

Mix	2½ cups finely crushed vanilla wafers
Well	1 cup confectioners' sugar (sifted)
	1 cup finely chopped nuts (walnut or filberts)
Add &	3 Tbsp. corn syrup
Mix	¼ cup Brandy

Roll into walnut size balls and then roll in powdered sugar. Let stand at least 24 hours and keep in tightly covered tin. Chocolate Brandy Balls: You may make a second batch with 2 Tbsp. powdered cocoa added to the dry mixture.
(3 dozen cookies)

To make your Holiday season festive, serve brandy balls. These should be made ahead of time to allow the full flavor to ripen.

Appetizer Cheezies

Cream	½ cup butter or margarine
Add	½ pound finely grated sharp cheese
Mix in	½ tsp. powdered Italian herbs
	½ tsp. onion salt
	½ tsp. celery salt
Sift in	1 cup flour

Work with a wooden paddle-type spoon. Mix with hands and roll into balls. Flatten with table knife. Brush with egg white and place salted peanut (or any type cocktail nut) on top. Bake at 375F for 7-10 minutes. Watch closely.
(4 dozen cookies)

Serve this appetizer right out of the oven with cocktails or soup. Freeze them ahead of time if you like, but allow five minutes for thawing.

Monterey Bizcochos

Cream	½ cup butter or margarine
Add	½ pound Monterey Jack cheese (grated)
Mix in	½ tsp. Chili powder
	½ tsp. oregano
	½ tsp. onion salt
	½ tsp. garlic salt

Sift in 1 cup flour

Work with wooden paddle-type spoon. Mix with hands and roll into balls. Flatten with table knife. Brush with egg white and place a nut (a salted pumpkin seed or pepito if possible) on the top. Bake at 375F for 7-10 minutes. Like Appetizer Cheezies these can be made ahead and put in freezer section. Take out for five minutes. You can roll the dough into sticks about 6 inches long for freezer. Such a stick will make a dozen bizcochos.
(4 dozen cookies)

Planning a Mexican Fiesta? Es un apetitivo grande with any beverage.

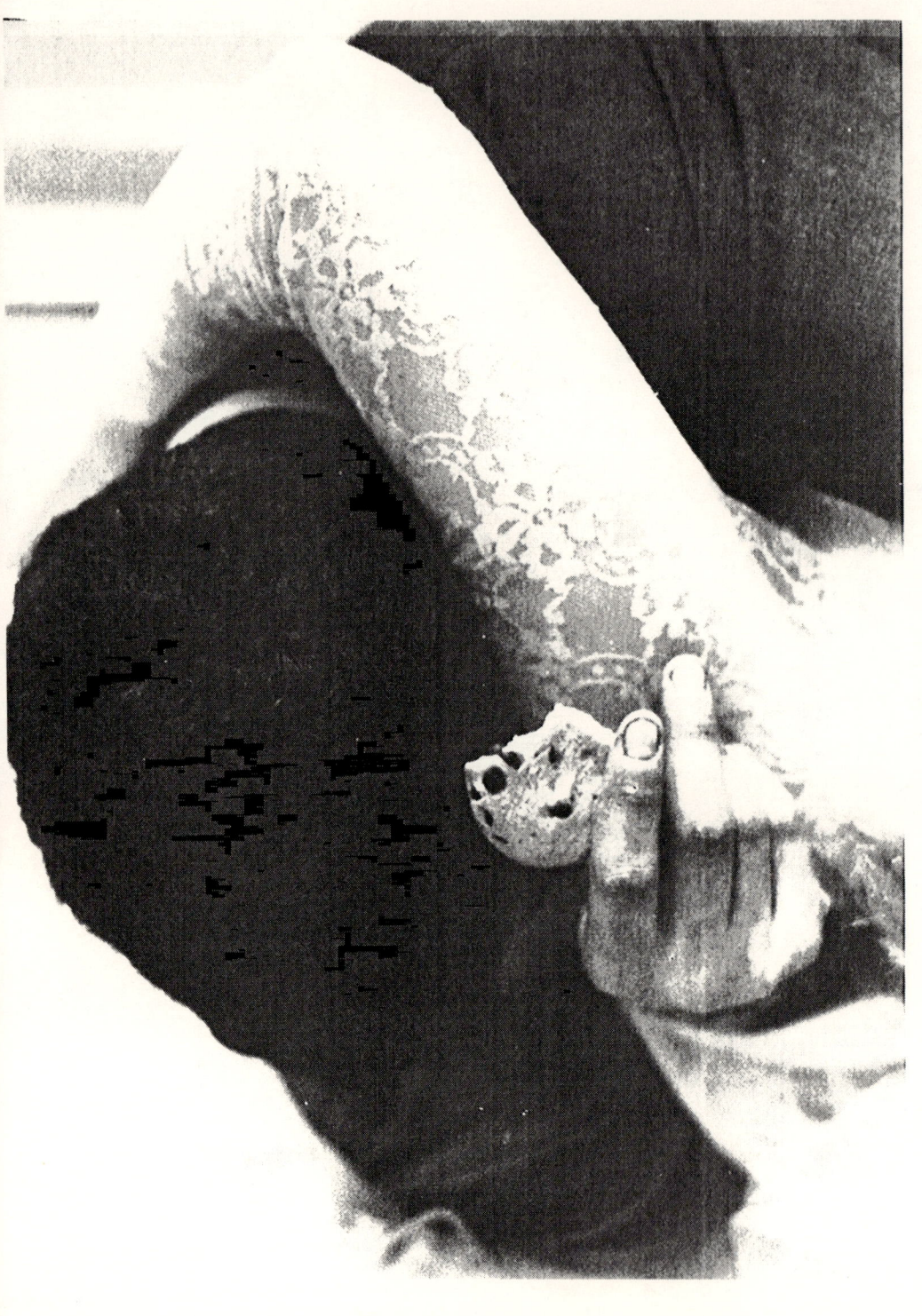

What Equals What

3 teaspoons	1 tablespoon
2 tablespoons	1 fluid ounce
16 tablespoons	1 cup
1 cup	.8 fluid ounces
1 juiced lemon	2-3 tablespoons
5 large eggs (approximately)	1 cup
1 square chocolate	1 ounce
2 cups butter	1 pound
2 cups granulated sugar	1 pound
2-2/3 cups confectioners' sugar	1 pound
2-2/3 cups brown sugar	1 pound
4 cups flour	1 pound
2 cups nut meats	½ pound
1 cup dates (cut)	½ pound
1-2/3 cups peanut butter	1 pound
3 cups raisins	1 pound
5 cups coconut	1 pound

Gilding the Lily - Icings and Frostings

Simple Confectioners' Frosting - Sift 2 cups confectioners' sugar. Gradually add ¼ cup milk and blend until smooth.

Rich Butter Icing - Blend together 3 Tbsp. soft butter, 1 egg yolk, 2 cups confectioners' sugar, 2 Tbsp. cream, 1 tsp. vanilla. Omit vanilla and use orange or lemon juice in place of cream for variation.

Golden Icing - Heat ¼ cup butter over low heat until golden. Stir in 1 cup of sifted confectioners' sugar and ½ tsp. vanilla. Add hot water until mixture is of spreading consistency.

Chocolate Frosting - Combine 2 squares of unsweetened chocolate, ¼ cup milk, 1 Tbsp. butter in top of double boiler. Heat and blend. Remove from heat. Add 1 cup sifted confectioners' sugar. Beat until smooth.

Peppermint Icing - Substitute 1 tsp. peppermint flavoring for vanilla in butter icing.

Decorating Icing - Sift 1 cup confectioners' sugar. Stir in 1 Tbsp. water or just enough to force through pastry tube. Put in drops of food coloring for desired tint.

Mocha-Butter Icing - Add 3 Tbsp. cocoa with confectioners' sugar; substitute strong hot coffee for other liquid.

How to Vary Everything or Substitutions

1 cup sifted flour	1 cup 2 Tbsp. Cake flour
1 tsp. baking powder	¼ tsp. soda and ½ tsp. cream of tartar
1 whole egg	2 yolks and 1 Tbsp. water
1 cup sour milk	1 cup sweet milk and 1 Tbsp. vinegar
1 cup sour milk	1 cup buttermilk
1 square chocolate	3 Tbsp. carob powder & 2 Tbsp. water
1 cup honey	¾ cup sugar and ½ cup liquid
1 cup sugar	1 cup honey and reduce liquid by ¼ cup
1 cup milk	3 Tbsp. powdered milk and 1 cup water

To make one-half recipe: Use exactly ½ of each ingredient except 1 egg. To double recipe: Use exactly twice amount and use pans accordingly to preserve depth of bar cookies.

Index

After School Cookies (Raisins-Cinnamon) 86
Allen's All Americans 155
Almond Butter Balls 70
Almond Macaroons, The Other 66
Almond Spritz, Very 138
Appetizer Chéezies 174
Armenian Cookies 105
Barbary Coast Cookies 161
Bar Cookies Instructions 71
Banana-Honey Bumps 25
Berry Yous 163
Birthday Party Cookies 17
Breakfast Cookies 43
Bride's Kisses 38
Brandy Balls 173
Brownies, Charlie's 77
Brownies, Family 74
Brownies, Status 75
Brownie Spoonfuls 165
Brunch Cookies 63
Butterscotch Flings 61
Cake n' Candy Cookies 101
California Raisin Balls 53
Carmel Carmelos 90
Carob Bean Islands 19
Carob Chip Cookies 11
Carob Puffs 41
Cashew Treats 46
Celebration Cookies 129
Chocolate Chippies 151
Chocolate Fudgies 18
Chocolate Munchies 57

Chocolate Spiral Cookies	150
Christmas Treats	54
Classic Sugar Cookies	37
Cinnamon Circles	157
Coconut Nutties	65
Coconut Shaggies	55
Coffee Toffees	45
Cracker Box Date Bars	93
Cream Cheese Cut Outs	118
Divine Date Balls	89
Desert Date Rocks	62
Drop Cookies Instructions	10
El Camino Orange Drops	146
Energy Cookies	30
Equivalents	176
Et Cetera Cookies	162
Feather Flakes	139
Fruit Filled Cookies	126
Fruit Fillings	127
Gingerbreadmen	125
Gingersnaps, Pioneer	122
Gingersnips	141
Glamaroos	169
Glenn's Grooveys	82
Groom's Choice Cookies	85
Gumdrop Slices	154
Happy Holiday Bars	102
Hibernation Cookies	99
Homespun Oatmeal Cookie	27
Honey Hermits	23
Honey Hugs	29
Honey Holly Wreaths	123

Hop Scotch Squares	83
Icings	178
Jam Bars	106
Jamey Pies	58
Karma Cookies	49
Keeping Cookies	9
Kindness Cookies	73 & 133
Lacy Doilies	33
Laurie's Loves (Butter Nut Crescents)	50
Lemon Drops (Greg's)	15
Lemon Loverlies	115
Little Angels	166
Luau Cookies	81
Macaroons, Elegante	34
Mandarin Chocolate Bites	13
Maple Nut Marvels	153
Meditation Bread	97
Meringues, Hollywood	35
Milk Chocolate Almond Bars	78
Mincemeat Miracles	158
Mission Fig Bars	95
Molded Cookies Instructions	47
Monterey Bizcochos	175
More Instant Cookies	170
Navidados	51
Nob Hill Cookies	171
Now Cookies (appetizers)	42
Open Sesames	103
Orange Blossom Bars	87
Orgy Makers	121
Pans	5
Panocha Cookies	79
Paper Dollies	114

Parmesan Sticks	142
Peanut Butter Spritz	145
Peanut Palominos	39
Peanut Pinwheels	119
Pecan Bars	98
Pennywise Cookies	134
Persimmon Cookies	21
Piñonitas (Pine Nut Cookies)	69
Pooh's Honey Cakes	91
Pressed Cookies Instructions	**135**
Prune Pickups	107
Pumpkin Eaters	22
Refrigerator Cookies Instructions	**147**
Rescue Cookies	149
Rice Almond Cakes	67
Rolled Cookies Instructions	**109**
Rolled Sugar Cookies (Basic)	111
Rolled Sugar Cookies Dresses Up	113
Rolled Sugar Cookie Times Six	110
Saucy Apple Cookies	26
Shortbread, Scotch	117
Shortbread, American Style	59
Sour Cream Bars	143
Substitutions	**179**
Sutters' Gold Nuggets	31
Sydney Biscuits	14
Vanilla Spritz	137
Vibration Cookies	130
Walnut Torte Cookies	131
Wilshire Tea Time	159
Zippity Zoos	167
Zwieback Date Layers	94

PHOTOGRAPHY BY:

Robert W. Cromey

J. L. Gerstein

J. W. Lentz

S. McCreary

Dennis Schmidling

Vince Sciortino

Craig Torlucci

Gary Zimmerman

Addendum

Since this book was first published there has been some innovations and inventions to be found in the cooking hardware department. Here are a few that will help in cookie making.

I now use a food processor. I have three sizes. The smallest is used for preparing nuts in the recipes. The medium size does a good job crushing graham crackers and such. The medium and larger size bowls are good for creaming shortening and sugar. It is possible to mix cookie dough in the food processor from start to finish, i.e. Scotch Shortbread. I cream the butter and sugar together. Then I add the dry ingredients-a little at a time and keep whirling the dough until it forms a ball. This is the same method that I use to make dough for a pie crust.

I now use my microwave oven to soften butter for creaming and for melting butter and chocolate. It is easier than the double boiler method and gives a smoother consistency. I put hard brown sugar or solid honey in the microwave for just a few seconds. This brings the ingredients to a proper consistency for mixing with other ingredients.

Cookie sheets have improved. With insulated pans of all sizes you can achieve just the right shape and size for your cookies. I now use No Stick Vegetable Cooking Spray to prepare cookie sheets for drop cookies and rolled cookies. The bottoms don't burn and cookies slide off easily with the help of a wide plastic spatula. Cookies are golden brown on top and bottom. I also use the spray on other types of pans.

The weather, altitude and your oven will affect the baking time of all cookies. Some people like a softer cookie so remember that cookies continue to bake after they come out of the oven. It's all in how you and your family like their cookies.

Now nutrition advice is in favor of butter rather than margarine so I use it and prefer it for the taste and texture. Please yourselves. Because of an allergy some of my recipes use Carob powder. You may substitute powdered cocoa. For those allergic to wheat I have found Rice flour a good substitute, particularly in cookies that add nuts and raisins, i.e. Persimmon Cookies. Above all, the best cookies are the ones that are your own originals.

AUTHORS GUILD BACKINPRINT.COM EDITIONS are fiction and nonfiction works that were originally brought to the reading public by established United States publishers but have fallen out of print. The economics of traditional publishing methods force tens of thousands of works out of print each year, eventually claiming many, if not most, award-winning and one-time best-selling titles. With improvements in print-on-demand technology, authors and their estates, in cooperation with the Authors Guild, are making some of these works available again to readers in quality paperback editions. Authors Guild Backinprint.com Editions may be found at nearly all online bookstores and are also available from traditional booksellers. For further information or to purchase any Backinprint.com title please visit www.backinprint.com.

Except as noted on their copyright pages, Authors Guild Backinprint.com Editions are presented in their original form. Some authors have chosen to revise or update their works with new information. The Authors Guild is not the editor or publisher of these works and is not responsible for any of the content of these editions.

THE AUTHORS GUILD is the nation's largest society of published book authors. Since 1912 it has been the leading writers' advocate for fair compensation, effective copyright protection, and free expression. Further information is available at www.authorsguild.org.

Please direct inquiries about the Authors Guild and Backinprint.com Editions to the Authors Guild offices in New York City, or e-mail staff@backinprint.com.